T4-ANG-696

PITTSBURGH THEOLOGICAL MONOGRAPH SERIES

General Editor
DIKRAN Y. HADIDIAN

4

THE SAMARITAN PROBLEM

Studies in the Relationships of Samaritanism, Judaism, and Early Christianity

PITTSBURGH THEOLOGICAL MONOGRAPH SERIES

Already Published

1. *Rhetorical Criticism; essays in honor of James Muilenburg.* Edited by Jared J. Jackson and Martin Kessler. 1974

2. Francois C. Gérard: *The Future of the Church; the theology of renewal of Willem Adolf Visser't Hooft.* 1974

3. *Structural Analysis and Biblical Exegesis; interpretational essays* by R. Barthes, F. Bovon, F. J. Leenhardt, R. Martin-Achard and J. Starobinski. Translated by Alfred M. Johnson, Jr. 1974

4. John Bowman: *The Samaritan Problem; Studies in the Relationships of Samaritanism, Judaism and Early Christianity.* With a new introduction. Translated by Alfred M. Johnson. 1975

5. *The Tale of the Tell; archaeological studies by Paul W. Lapp.* Edited by Nancy L. Lapp. 1975

6. Donald E. Gowan: *When Man becomes God; Humanism and Hybris in the Old Testament.* 1975

Forthcoming

7. John Bowman: *The Fourth Gospel and the Jews; a study of R. Akibah, Esther, and the Gospel of John.* 1975

8. *The Informal Groups in the Church.* Papers of the Second Cerdic Colloquium. Strasbourg, May 13-15, 1971. Edited by René Metz and Jean Schlick. Translated by Matthew J. O'Connell. 1975

9. Jack M. Maxwell: *Worship and Reformed Theology; the liturgical lessons of Mercersburg.* 1975

10. Robert G. Heath: *Crux Imperatorum Philosophia: Imperial Horizons of the Cluniac Liturgical Community, 964-1109.* 1975

11. *The New Testament and Structuralism,* a collection of essays edited by Alfred M. Johnson, Jr. 1975

12. *Liberation Ideaology and the Message of Salvation.* Papers of the Fourth Cerdic Colloquium. Strasbourg, May 10-12. Edited by René Metz and Jean Schlick. Translated by David Gelzer. 1976

13. Louis Marin: *The Semiotic of the Passion Narratives.* Translated by Alfred M. Johnson, Jr. 1976

14. Richard Reitzenstein: *The Hellenistic Mystery Religions.* Translated by John Steely. 1976

THE SAMARITAN PROBLEM

Studies in the Relationships of Samaritanism, Judaism, and Early Christianity

Franz Delitzsch Lectures 1959

by

JOHN BOWMAN

Translated

by

ALFRED M. JOHNSON, JR.

THE PICKWICK PRESS

PITTSBURGH, PENNSYLVANIA

1975

Originally published in 1967 as *Samaritanische Probleme; Studien zum Verhältnis von Samaritanertum, Judentum und Urchristentum.*

Library of Congress Cataloging in Publication Data

Bowman, John, 1916-
The Samaritan problem.

(Franz Delitzsch lectures ; 1959) (Pittsburgh theological monograph series ; no. 4)
Translation of Samaritanische Probleme.
Includes bibliographical references.
1. Samaritans--Religion. 2. Christianity and other religions--Samaritanism. 3. Qumran community. I. Title. II. Series. III. Series: Pittsburgh theological monograph series ; no. 4.
BM935.B6413 296.8'1 75-20042
ISBN 0-915138-04-2

TABLE OF CONTENTS

[illegible]

TRANSLATOR'S FOREWARD

The cover of this book requires some description. At the suggestion of Dr. Bowman, we have "clothed" this work in a Samaritan phylactery (cf. Mtt. 23:5). According to Dr. Bowman, the Samaritans believed that by wearing such phylacteries they were literally "putting on the Word of God". Further discussions on these phylacteries are found in the bibliography at the end of this volume.

Dr. Bowman was also kind enough to supply us with two photos of a Samaritan Decalogue inscription which were taken in 1950. Although this inscription is not discussed in this work, these photos are clear proof, if any is needed, for the existence of contacts between the Christian and Samaritan communities, which is what *The Samaritan Problem* is all about. For a more detailed discussion of this inscription see the article by Dr. Bowman (*The Bulletin of John Rylands Library* 33 [1950/51], pp. 217-218).

I would like to express my gratification in playing a small role in translating into English this work which, according to some scholars, is considered to be the best introductory work available on the Samaritans. At present I have in my possession a new work by Dr. Bowman on the gospel of John which will hopefully appear later this year in this series. I will not disclose its contents except to say that it one of the most fascinating studies of the Fourth Gospel which I have ever read.

The scholarly value of *The Samaritan Problem* is confirmed by the fact that, although it was written almost a decade ago, no major changes were needed to bring it up to date. In it the New Testament scholar will find many new materials and interpretations which were previously inaccessible in English. For despite all the work which has been done by Dr. Bowman and others on the Samaritans, New Testament scholars persist in following outworn and trite evaluations of the Samaritans as extreme right-wing "pseudo-Jews" who by their exclusion of the Prophets and Writings from their canon could not possibly have been of great influence on Jesus, his disciples, or the Early Church. Hopefully this work will further help to shatter such prejudices as these which might still exist.

In _The Samaritan Problem_ one enters a world which is foreign to the New Testament scholar. From Arabic and Hebrew Samaritan sources one begins to see how the Zadokites, Nazirites, Dositheans, Gnostics, and Samaritan sectarians fit into the overall picture of the milieu in which Jesus and his disciples lived. As far as I am aware, this work gives us, for the first time in English, a detailed discussion of the beliefs and practices of these groups which have perplexed biblical scholars for so long. For those who have been following the debate presently surrounding the Samaritan origin of Stephen's speech in Acts 7, it should be noted that Dr. Bowman has provided us with a translation of that Arabic passage from Abu'l Faṭh which has been so often cited but never translated (see n. 9, p. 137).

The major problems which arose in this translation concerned a consistent system of transliterating the Hebrew and Arabic names which appear throughout this work. As one will note from the foreword to the German edition, this was a problem which also plagued the first edition. Where possible, I have tried to retain the most easily recognizable spelling of names which appear in the biblical materials familiar to the New Testament scholar (i.e., the Bible, the Dead Sea Scrolls, Philo, Josephus, the Apocrypha and Pseudepigrapha, etc.). However, although the biblical priest Phinehas (Num. 25:7; Jos. 22:13, et al.) has the same name as the Samaritan priest named herein Phineas, I have reserved the name Phineas for the latter and Phinehas for the former in order to differentiate them as they were in the German original. Likewise names that have appeared in other English works on the Samaritans (e.g., by Bowman, Macdonald, Gaster, et al.) were made to conform to such precedents as existed. The only problem with this approach was that the precedents themselves differed! Therefore, I have favored Macdonald's usage in his The Theology of the Samaritans, because it is well-known to most biblical scholars and it was the latest comprehensive work on the Samaritans I had at hand. It would be of great service to scholars in this area if someone could devise a consistent system of transliterations for the Hebrew, Arabic, and Greek names which could be used by all biblical scholars internationally. Until such a system appears, however, we will be forced to do the best we can. Dr. Bowman did, however, read the entire translation and made helpful suggestions concerning this and other problems which were utilized.

It remains only for me to thank Dr. Bowman for allowing me to translate and publish this work of his and also to thank him for the materials, kind advice, and criticism which he provided throughout. I must also thank a good friend, Mrs. Alice Davis, who helped me find English equivalents for a number of difficult German idioms and also my typist, Ms. Kathy A. Herrin whose careful work never ceases to amaze me. Finally, I must thank the editor of this series, Dikran Y. Hadidian, for publishing this work and for the invaluable assistance which he, as always, provided.

Alfred M. Johnson, Jr.

University of Pittsburgh
April 1, 1975

NEW INTRODUCTION TO THE ENGLISH EDITION

It is a year since Alfred M. Johnson, Jr. wrote to me and told me that he had translated my _Samaritanische Probleme_ from the German and wished to publish his English translation. I gladly consented, subject to the approval of Kohlhammer--the German publisher--and Professor Rengstorf of the Institutum Judaicum Delitzschianum, Munster University. It was in 1959 at the invitation of Professor Rengstorf that I delivered the four lectures which were afterwards published by Kohlhammer as _Samaritanische Probleme_ with the subtitle: _Studien zum Verhältnis von Samaritanertum, Judentum und Urchristentum_. It is this fact (that the lectures sought to deal with the relationship of Samaritanism, Judaism, and Early Christianity, and not only with Samaritanism) that justify their being reprinted in an English edition sixteen years after they were first delivered, and nine years after being first printed in German.

My approach to Samaritan studies was largely shaped by getting to know the present state of the Samaritans' religion today, listening to their claims as to its orthodoxy, antiquity and unchangeableness, and then working back from the known present. Three things are important: (1) Their Bible, the Samaritan Pentateuch; (2) Their ancestral priesthood who are "Cohens" still in more than mere name; and (3) Their liturgy.

Apart from Islam, religion in the Middle East has tended to be or become ethnic. This applies not only to Jews and Samaritans, but to Christian sects like the Nestorians or

Assyrians and the Armenians. Even in Islam, religion fostered a sense of nationality. With the Samaritans, while we do not necessarily exclude their tradition of descent from the Northern Israelites, religious separatism worked to strengthen their ethnic separation from the Jews. But in religion they and the Jews still have the Torah as the common symbol of their respective faiths. Granted the Samaritan Pentateuch has two significant differences from the Jewish Pentateuch: (a) the special Samaritan Tenth Commandment as to where God's altar is to be (at Mt. Gerizim not Mt. Zion) and (b) there shall not arise another, a prophet like Moses (Sam. Targum Deut. 34:10). Here in a nutshell is Samaritanism over against Judaism: Mt. Gerizim over against Mt. Zion (Jerusalem); _one_ Holy Book, the Pentateuch, given by one prophet Moses--as over against the Law and the Prophets and the Holy Writings (including the Psalms of David) which together make up the threefold canon of Jewish Scripture. But the Pentateuch in its final form is post-exilic and is more about Moses than by Moses.

Certainly then Samaritanism in its earliest form is post-exilic, and the separation probably took place in the early 4th century B.C. at the earliest. We would not be wrong in fixing the time of the schism with the casting out of the Jerusalem high priest's grandson who was married to the daughter of Sanballat (Neh. 13:28), and the covenanting of the people to keep the Law (cf. Neh. 9) in the presence of Ezra. But the Prophets and the Holy Writings were not included in this covenant. Only by use and wont were they later accepted in Jewish synagogue worship; and the Palestinian Hebrew canon was not fixed till the last quarter of the 1st century A.D.

The Samaritan high priest at his altar and temple on Mt. Gerizim (Shechem) doubtless held fast to the Law and did not allow any change. He was not a schismatic, he had been thrown out for marrying out; he was not a reformer, he wanted to hold to the past. But he did make a virtue of necessity. There was only one prophet--Moses, and one place to worship God--Mt. Gerizim (i.e. Bethel, "the House of God"); and after all _that_ strengthened his priesthood. One would not be surprised that despite the immediate founder of the Samaritan high priesthood's marrying out, subsequent Samaritan high priests stressed their genealogy. It was their claim to that position and power. Hence a basic document in Samaritan research is the _Tolidah_--or genealogy of the high priests with notes on significant events, if any, in their time of office.

So much for Law and Priesthood; there remains Liturgy. There are two volumes of it published by A. E. Cowley (_Samaritan Liturgy_, Oxford, 1909). None of this can be proved to be earlier than the 4th century A.D. (apart from the scripture readings and catena which Cowley did not print) and most of it is post-14th century A.D. Even in the material from the 4th century A.D., there are doctrines and views which would be unheard of to the priestly founding-fathers of Samaritanism in the 4th century B.C.

We know from Josephus (_Antiquities of the Jews_, XIII, §254f.) that John Hyrcanus destroyed the Samaritan Temple on Mt. Gerizim in the latter part of the second century B.C. This must have weakened the Samaritan priesthood's hold over the community. There is evidence from Josephus (_Ibid_., XVIII, §85-89) of Samaritan messianism and how Pontius Pilate dealt with it to his downfall. From Church Fathers like Origen (_Contra Celsum_, VI, 2) as well as from much later Samaritan sources like the Tolidah and the Samaritan Annals of Abu'l Fatḥ, we learn of sectarian divisions which seem to be grouped under the omnibus title of Dositheism. The Clementine Recognitions (2, 8) say that Dositheus was the pupil (and teacher!) of Simon Magus, but his actual date is uncertain. He or the group that took, or was given, his name seem to have represented developments in Judaism in the later intertestamental period and early Christian centuries. Origen in his Commentary on John's Gospel (XIII, 27--on Jn. 4:25) says that a certain Dositheus of the Samaritans came forward and said that he was the prophesied Christ. Origen adds that "from that day to this" there are Dositheans who say that he did not taste death, but is still alive!

In the 4th century A.D. there was a big change at Nablus (the ancient Shechem). Inter alia, the power and status of the priesthood was curtailed, but it survived. There seems to have been a coming to terms between some of the old priestly group and the party of change, i.e. the Dositheans, under Baba Rabba--the then high priest. It was in his time that Marqah and Amram Darah compiled their hymns for the Liturgy, which reflected the new spirit and new teachings.

After Baba's death there is a revival of the old priestly power. Doctrines in the writings of the fourth century are set aside till practically one thousand years later when there is another, and this time lasting, attempt at oecumenism between the ultra-conservative priestly power and the Dositheans. It is then that the great Samaritan Liturgies were written full of teachings which recall those of the 4th century experiment in oecumenism. But this time they go much further, e.g. Dositheus according to Origen (Contra Celsum, VI, 2) had set himself up as the messiah foretold in Deut. 18:18. This, at least, means that Dositheus according to Origen was putting himself in place of Moses. Whether Origen's knowledge of the use of Deut. 18:18 in John's gospel has influenced his allegation of Dositheus claiming messiahship, and this be a reference to the Samaritan Taheb, or Dositheus himself made the claim, cannot be resolved here. If the latter did, it is less of a claim than that of his teacher, Simon Magus, whom Hippolytus cites (Refutation of All Heresies, ch. XIII) as claiming to be the "Standing One", the Greek of which is a literal translation of הקום, a divine name in the Samaritan Liturgy (cf. also Clement Alex., Strom., II). Actually in the Samaritan Liturgy we have the only clear identification of the Taheb and the one like Moses (Deut. 18:18) in a hymn on the Taheb of the 14th century at the time of what I see as the second Samaritan oecumenical movement, though the Taheb was known in the Memar Marqah in the 4th century. There is no reference to the Taheb in the Samaritan Pentateuch; for the old orthodox priestly group still believed that God acted directly: cf. Deut. 30:2 which states that if the Hebrew returned to the Lord and obeyed His covenantal commandments that then (v. 3) "the Lord thy God will turn thy captivity" (K.J.V. influenced by Targum Onkelos). The Targum Pseudo-Jonathan has "His Word will accept your repentance with favour". The Samaritan Targum has "that the Lord thy God may return with (עם) thy turning" (or conversion). It is noteworthy too that in the intervening 1,000 years (after the 4th century) in the Samaritan community the priestly writings do not know of the Taheb, cf. Hassan al-Suri's Kitab al-Tabaḫ (11th century); nor do they know of any return of Moses either. Only in the 4th century A.D. when the Samaritan community was at a very low ebb with declining numbers, the priests compromised again and accepted the Dosithean sect into their midst; and this time they accepted its doctrines even more explicitly. So what is now orthodox Samaritanism post-14th century may have been largely accepted into orthodoxy in the 14th century, but certainly it was not orthodox Samaritanism prior to the 4th century _nor_ between then and the 14th century.

This is the thesis set out in these lectures. The present writer finds in his continuing researches in Samaritan studies that this thesis holds good. Prof. J. Macdonald, a younger colleague of mine when we were at Leeds University, in his _The Theology of the Samaritans_ (London: SCM Press, 1964) would deny that Baba Rabba or Marqah had come to terms with Dositheism as part of an oecumenical movement. He really sets aside the problem of Marqah's relation, if any, to the Dositheans on the one hand and the conservative priestly group on the other. Baba and Marqah were orthodox for him. Dr. H. G. Kippenberg (_Garizim und Synagoge_, Berlin: de Gruyter, 1971) largely follows Prof. Macdonald and seems to allow for no development or change after the 4th century A.D., but he regards Samaritanism as static thereafter. Both ignore the contribution of Dositheism to orthodox Samaritanism as it now stands.

In these lectures I make critical use of the basic Samaritan historical materials. The present writer is aware that there are other Samaritan chronicles, especially some in Hebrew, which were not cited in these lectures. This is said here because of the renewed interest in such Hebrew chronicles aroused in recent years by Professor Macdonald and Dr. A. D. Crown. Despite Dr. Crown's learned articles on such Samaritan chronicles, e.g. in <u>The John Rylands Bulletin</u> 54 (1972), pp. 282-313, one judges it is still safer today to draw one's conclusions from the Tolidah; the Samaritan Arabic Book of Joshua; and Abu'l Fatḥ's <u>Samaritan Annals</u>. But it is essential that the original Tolidah text, as preserved in the high priest's house in Nablus, be used and not that of Neubauer's edition which latter takes up into the text marginalia and other later glosses. One was disappointed that Dr. Crown still used Neubauer's conflated text when discussing the value of the Tolidah in the aforementioned article; but one was gratified to see the importance he put on the Arabic version of the Samaritan Joshua.

Nothing that is said in the following lectures claims to be final. There is no final solution to the Samaritan Problem, whether it be their own history, or the history of their religion--and one cannot think of one apart from the other. There are no clearcut answers to the relationships which existed between Samaritanism, Judaism, Early Christianity and the Qumran Sect. These lectures indicate the problems and postulate theories which open doors to future research.

It remains for me to venture to compliment Mr. A. M Johnson, Jr. on his easy reading English translation of the German edition.

John Bowman

Dept. of Middle Eastern Studies
University of Melbourne
Parkville 3052
Victoria, Australia
Jan. 29, 1975

FOREWORD TO THE GERMAN EDITION

The publication of the Franz Delitzsch Lectures of 1959 has been unusually delayed for a number of reasons. Soon after Professor Bowman delivered these lectures from his academic position at the University of Leeds, he accepted a call to the University of Melbourne, where he took over the chairmanship of the Department of Semitic Studies. This change of position and the great distance connected with it proved to be a troublesome obstacle to overcome with respect to the preparations (which had begun very soon after their delivery) for the printing of these lectures. This was especially true since these lectures were delivered from a provisional translation whose revision was planned from the beginning.

The troublesome and time-consuming work which was involved in the production of this text for printing was done under my supervision essentially by my assistant pastor, Arnulf Baumann, S.T.M. My colleague Mrs. Ruth Schröder (born: Klusmann) assisted him in the editing and prepared the typed manuscript. A theology student, Bernd Bierbaum, prepared the index. Rev. Baumann and Mr. Bierbaum also helped in the corrections. All of them well deserve the gratitude of the editor and also that of the author.

It should be pointed out that new publications appearing after 1959 could only be referred to occasionally and then only in the notes. Uniformity in the transliterations with regard to the spelling of the proper names could not be perfectly attained.

I am pleased that this combined effort has succeeded and that this gap in the series of the Franz Delitzsch Lectures, which I regretted many times, has finally ended; and thus the theses of a scholar which have received much praise in the area of Samaritan research (an area which has received comparatively little attention) have also been made accessible to a wider audience in the German language.

Karl Heinrich Rengstorf

Munster in the Summer of 1966
Institutum Judaicum Delitzschianum

CHAPTER I

"The History of the Samaritans" [p.9]

Today there are approximately 360 Samaritans. Most of them live in Nablus, the remainder in Holon in Tel Aviv-Jaffa. The Samaritans have a long history. Unfortunately their own historical records are sparse and confused. Therefore it is difficult to reconstruct with any accuracy a Samaritan history from the Samaritan historical tradition. To be sure there are still Samaritans! But are they exactly like their forefathers? Without a doubt, Samaritanism originated at some time--but when, where and how? All these are controversial questions.

What the biblical, Jewish, Christian, and Muslim sources offer to us about the Samaritans is not only fragmentary but also polemic and, in addition, filled with contradictions. On the other hand, Samaritan historical writing is apologetic and does not always arouse confidence with regard to its reliability. Thus the study of Samaritan history is more complicated than one generally assumes. But it is rewarding; for this much insulted and frequently misunderstood community has preserved ancient conceptions of faith and customs which can cast much light both on the intertestamental period and on the background of the New Testament.

Naturally I cannot cover the entire Samaritan history, but I must limit myself to the time periods which are meaningful to us today. Therefore I will have to depend continuously upon the customs and faith of contemporary Samaritans in order to replenish our fragmentary knowledge about the past. In defense I can only state that the Samaritan sect is generally conservative. They are therefore inclined to incorporate heresies and schisms into their community instead of removing them. Thus the heresies frequently remain "undigested", as will be shown in later arguments.

For my part I can also state that there is not much continuity between the contemporary Samaritan faith and the ancient religion of Northern Israel. To be sure a connection exists here, but it is hardly a direct one. It is therefore extremely difficult to trace the connecting lines from the political and social history of the kingdom of Northern Israel to the post-exilic Samaritan community. That is not to say that there are none, but nevertheless we must admit in our present state of knowledge that we do not know about them. [p.10] In any case, it is unlikely that all the inhabitants of the Northern Kingdom were deported in the year 721 B.C. That is not even asserted by the prejudiced report in 2 Kings 17. Also all of the tribes which were colonized there from Assyria did not necessarily come into the country at that point in time. The history of the territory which had belonged to the Northern Kingdom is obscure in the period between 721 B.C. and the middle of the 5th century A.D. It is possible that the circumstances there after the fall of Samaria were not very different from the situation in Judah after the fall of Jerusalem, the only difference being that foreign elements established themselves in the North of their own volition. (In the South the worship of God on the altar at Jerusalem probably continued, but the inhabitants of the country no longer agreed with the new, stricter interpretation of the Yahweh faith held by the returning Jews. One should not forget that this new rigoristic group probably stands behind 2 Kings 17, with its invectives toward the inhabitants of Northern Israel. Since these Northerners did not have the "advantage" of having been in the Babylonian captivity and furthermore, since they came from the North, they were treated very contemptuously by the former Exiles.) Assyrians, Babylonians, and Persians one after another ruled the North; the last two also ruled the South. However, we do not know any details of the Babylonian and Persian rule in their own province even from the Jewish side, except for the time when Sanballat was the Persian governor in Shechem.

From the time of the Exile we know of two attempts by which the kingdom of Judah tried to exercise its power over the northern territory. The first attempt was in the time of Hezekiah;[1] the other was in the time of Josiah.[2] The biblical tale stressed the purely religious aspect of both occupations. But religion and politics were closely connected to one another in the ancient Orient and could not be neatly separated. What effect Hezekiah and Josiah had on the North is not known. Nevertheless, Jeremiah testifies that a few inhabitants of Northern Israel brought sacrifices to the altar of the previously destroyed Jerusalem temple.[3] The report about Hezekiah and Josiah also mentions that part of the house of Joseph remained in the North in the 7th century B.C. However, the biblical sources say nothing about the fate of the inhabitants of the Northern Kingdom during the Babylonian occupation of Palestine. A remnant of Israelites probably still lived in the North towards the end of the 7th century B.C. They were still there about the end of the 6th century B.C. when a few of the Jews who had been deported to Babylon returned. However, they may have assimilated themselves to the Jews who remained in Judea. But it is more likely that the latter would have united themselves with the Israelites that remained in the North for [p.11] these Northerners meanwhile had had more experience in surviving the yoke of foreign rule.

From the biblical reports it does not necessarily follow that the enemies of the returning Jews were Samaritans.[4] On the whole, it is questionable whether this term existed at that time. Only this much is clear--the land was not deserted and the returning Jews only had permission to settle around Jerusalem and to rebuild their temple there. Toward the end of the 6th century they dreamed of the kingdom of David being permitted to be reborn again, but that never happened. Later the goal was to establish a theocratic state. Nevertheless, half a century passed before the walls of Jerusalem were rebuilt. Meanwhile the inhabitants of the Northern Kingdom, the ones who had ruled Palestine for the Persians up to that time, became restless (as can be concluded from the report of Sanballat's interference in Nehemiah).[5] Probably Nehemiah's wall was mainly intended to protect the Temple. If this was the case, then Ezra only acted consistently when he excluded those who did not belong to the group of the former Babylonian exiles, as well as those exiles who married the resident Jews or Samaritans. Ezra successfully erected in and around Jerusalem a small but compact and homogeneous religious state, which, to be sure, was not independent and was scarcely able to maintain itself. It was of great advantage to him that he could show the Persian governors that his Jews were different from all the others. Thus religion and politics stood beside one another in a close reciprocal relationship. For Ezra and his followers, they themselves and no others were the true Israel. As for the Rabbis of the Mishnaic period, it was inconceivable that the name Israel could be applied to anyone outside of their own adherents. But even if Ezra and his followers, by stressing the alleged difference between the inhabitants of the country and the Samaritans, curtailed the power of Sanballat and the ruling class in Shechem, the Northerners and the Samaritans under Sanballat had more power in Palestine during the entire Persian period than the Jews of Jerusalem simply because the lieutenant-governor [p.12] ruled from Shechem. The remainder of the house of Joseph, along with the opponents of Jerusalem, and the ones excluded during the lifetime of Ezra outnumbered the Jews of Jerusalem even up until the time of the Greeks.

Therefore the discord between the North and South did not end with the destruction of the Northern Kingdom in the year 721, but it was renewed again by the return of the different groups of religiously zealous Jews from Babylon. Once again as the returning Southerners forced a division and a breach, this division lasted continuously during the Greek and Roman times. Indeed it is true that after the Maccabean revolt the supremacy of the South was restored for some time, especially by the attack of Hyrcanus on Shechem,[6] but only a few of his conquests could be held. While Galilee became Jewish and the Southern district of Ephraim went to Judah,[7] Samaria remained a district unto itself, although it was ruled by the Romans together with Judea.[8] Since Herod took Sebaste in Samaria to be his seat of government, this strengthened the power of the Samaritans. Galilean pilgrims on the way to Jerusalem considered it dangerous to pass through the province of Samaria which was for them to some extent an enemy foreign country.[9] Although a

Samaritan revolt first had to be put down during the war of 70 A.D., this revolt had nothing to do with the Roman-Jewish war. After the destruction of Jerusalem, Palestine was again governed from Vespasian's new city Neapolis/Nablus (formerly Shechem).[10] However during the Hadrianic wars, the Samaritans attached themselves to the general revolt[11] and also suffered as a result of Hadrian's victory. But in spite of religious persecution, they continued to exist as an ethnic group during the later time of the pagan gentile Roman empire, during the Christian empire, and even after the Caesar Zeno had destroyed the temple which was built upon Mount Gerizim in the time of Hadrian.

The edict of Justinian I against the Manicheans, Samaritans, and other heretics probably had the effect of finally eliminating the Samaritans as a [p.13] power faction.[12] Possibly Justinian probably attacked them just as much because of their treasonable relationship to the Persians as well as their tough adherence to their religious convictions and customs. I do not want to pursue the particular fortunes or misfortunes to which the Samaritans were exposed under the Persians/Parthians and the Muslims. Under the latter their situation worsened in the 2nd millennium A.D. since they were caught in the middle of groups of Crusaders and Muslims who were fighting against one another. Later they were overrun by the Mongols and Turks.[13] The fact that they survived all of this is evidence of their will to live and the unshakable strength of this last remnant of the lineage of Joseph.

Nevertheless, these irrefutably stalwart Israelites have not been as successful in overcoming the storms of their ever changing history as their Jewish brothers. They were the first to endure national humiliation which even Judah did not escape, although a forewarning of a similar fate had been bestowed on it by the destruction of the Northern Kingdom. (To be sure, the best minds in Judah learned from the destruction of the North to be prepared for the shock of the Exile, and thus they were able to prepare themselves during the Exile for the day of the return with all the self-discipline which the Exile could give them.) The remnant of the Northern Kingdom which remained behind in the country was never again infused with new blood by a mass return of prisoners. Indeed when the Jews returned from Babylon, the Northerners and those who would later be called Samaritans possessed a political advantage because they were in possession of the land. We will later see[14] how the Babylonian Exile led indirectly to a certain revival even for the Samaritans by some of the returnees and by the Torah in the form in which it returned from Babylon. But although this Torah was grafted upon in the North, it remained in the possession of the priests who had brought it from the South when Ezra expelled Sanballat's son-in-law from Jerusalem.[15] A lay community of the Torah, which considered the Law to be its property, could not have developed at the same time. Even in Greek and Roman times the situation of the Samaritans was apparently more favorable than that of the Jews. Nevertheless, in the end the Jews and not the Samaritans were favored with good fortune. That came about partly because the latter held fast to Shechem and Mount Gerizim while the Jews henceforth prayed at the wailing wall.

Like the Jews the Samaritans also had their Diaspora.[16] Both groups were [p.14] approximately equally represented in Alexandria. In addition, there were Samaritans in Damascus,

Babylon, Rome, and Constantinople. A Samaritan Diaspora existed in Egypt and Syria from antiquity until the 18th century. The sect was and is robust, but it is also conservative and inflexible. Therefore its losses were always greater than those of Judaism. In spite of the dispersion of the sect, no transfer of priestly duties into the Diaspora was permitted, although the priests were the scholars and intellectuals of the sect. The whole organism was and remained completely aligned to Nablus as its central point. (Moreover, considering the various fates of Nablus, it is amazing that Samaritan records are still preserved at all.)

On the other hand, the Jewish communities were all autonomous; for the Mishnah and later the Talmud presented firm rules for every possible event of life which was not taken into consideration in the Torah. After the end of the Talmudic era the systems of She'elot and Teshubot (community questions and the decisions of famous individual scholars) helped to complete or explain the Talmudic rules. So, for example, on the basis of a decision of a Rabbi of the 11th century,[17] the question of polygamy or monogamy among the Jews of Christian Europe was settled by a binding decision in favor of monogamy.

Judaism owes its development to oral teaching. Samaritanism, on the other hand, stuck closely to the dead letter of the written law. So in spite of gentile attacks on different Jewish centers of culture through the centuries, Judaism was able to survive no doubt thanks to its smaller, compact but more effective organization. Even though it lost its temple priesthood in 70 A.D., it nevertheless gained a priesthood of all believers, who all had the same interest in upholding Judaism and who also had a firm external foundation in the Jewish community relationship. However, the heart of Samaritanism was and remained the priesthood in Nablus, and its members could not leave the Holy Land without becoming at the same time unclean. Thus the Samaritan Diaspora in Alexandria, Damascus, or Rome was always in danger of feeling separated from the priestly stock in Nablus. Nevertheless, the priests refused to give up their power and to adapt Samaritan piety to the new circumstances. We will come back later to the consequences and results of this position for the Samaritan religion.[18]

Now it is time to turn to the Samaritan historical tradition. As already indicated, we shall consider a very difficult [p.15] point. The few Samaritan Annals which we know do contain historical statements. They are more important, however, as evidence of how particular Samaritans would like to portray other Samaritans both inside and outside the community. It has already been said that the Samaritan histories are full of anti-Jewish polemic. Thus it is much more difficult for Christians to judge the accuracy of the Samaritan assertions, since they are disciples of the one who said that salvation comes from the Jews[19] and whose Bible was the Jewish Old Testament. However, even if we take into consideration our inability to be entirely objective in this matter, anti-Jewish polemic still remains in Samaritan historical writing. Nevertheless Samaritanism did not escape the danger of putting a certain historical stamp on the Jewish narratives,[20] while incorporating them with slight changes into its own history. However, as an outsider, it is even more difficult for a Christian to evaluate the charges which appear in Samaritan sources against other Samaritans. Since many Samaritan manuscripts are available in European libraries, it has always remained a mystery to me why Christian scholars, who have known since the time of Joseph Scaliger[21] about the survival of the Samaritans, still repeat the same assertions about the Samaritans which were made by the Jews of post-Babylonian, Mishnaic and Talmudic times and which have come through the Church Fathers into the Christian scholarly tradition.

Here some remarks concerning the history of this research should be given. From 1616[22] up to the time of Wilhelm Gesenius,[23] interest in the Samaritans was concentrated on their version of the Pentateuch. In the 17th century the Samaritan Pentateuch was a good weapon for the Roman Catholic Church to use against all churches who maintained that the Bible alone was sufficient without the tradition of the church. The Samaritan Pentateuch had no Tiberian vocalization and deviated from the Jewish Hebrew text. But the two Buxtorfs[24] believed that the Jewish-Hebrew text together with the punctuation as it now exists may have been given on Mount Sinai. [p.16] Johannes Morinus,[25] who printed the Samaritan Pentateuch in his Parisian Polyglot, found in this version justification for his assertion that the Hebrew Bible could be interpreted as one pleased without punctuation and without the tradition of the church. When, in time, both sides changed their positions, interest in the Samaritan biblical text ceased. Gesenius and a few advocates of the young German science of Judaism then turned to the examination of the Samaritan liturgies and the Samaritan Midrashim. But their works, whose study is still worthwhile, had a very little effect on the scholarly views of Samaritan tradition. In the past few decades German scholars such as Joachim Jeremias, Albrecht Alt, and my old teacher Paul Kahle have also done much to advance the scholarly investigation of the Samaritans in Germany and to point out its significance for the study of the Old and New Testament.

The discoveries of Qumran have now induced some scholars to question the frequently used and all too easily accepted idea of "Normative Judaism" and the rabbinic sources as reliable criteria for the essence of Judaism of the 1st century. Consequently it appears to be appropriate once again to examine precisely whether or not the Samaritans, as the first Jewish sect who have no independent traditions and customs, have nevertheless preserved customs and views which are older than those which the Rabbis of the 2nd century A.D. (and later) tried to make sacrosanct by passing them off as oral traditions from the time of Moses that had been handed down to them as the trustees of the only and true Israel.

Now should one say that Christian and Jewish scholars are guilty of this one-sided picture of the Samaritans which has existed to the present day? Surely we cannot fully forgive ourselves for having permitted Samaritan material, which has been accessible for so long, to remain unexamined. However, even the Samaritan priests have not always been co-operative when it came to acquiring a better understanding of Samaritanism. Even if they no longer remember it today, the old Samaritan/Jewish-Christian antipathy is still being felt. Anti-Jewish polemic has become nothing short of the destiny of Samaritanism, and it has superseded everything else. If one speaks with Samaritan priests, reads the writings of Samaritans to European scholars, or examines the official Samaritan history books, then one easily gets the impression that Samaritanism has never changed and that the inner life of the sect, although it was constantly persecuted and ridiculed, is monotonous and dull. In any case, it appears at first glance to be only a petrified [p.17] nonconformist sect which once made unjustified claims and which has outlived its raison d'être, if indeed it ever possessed one. Later we will have more to say on this point. For the time being, it is enough to say that such an interpretation could not be further from the truth.

Samaritanism possesses an independent life. To be sure its essence is not immediately apparent. It is like those Samaritan houses which Petro della Valle saw in Damascus. They are shabby and dismal on the outside but beautiful and luxurious on the inside.[26] The reason why the Samaritans keep so much of their religious life a secret is, on the one hand, due to their non-conformist complex; but, on the other hand, it is also due to the priesthood. The priests are the guardians of the history and folklore of the sect, and today as from time immemorial they are jealously bent on safeguarding the holy mysteries. Accordingly they divulge only as much as is necessary in their opinion to harm the concerns of the Jews, or only as much as an outsider could understand. According to them, the tradition of the community is only for believers, not the whole tradition, but only as much as is necessary in order to support the priestly claims. What the priests let be known has always been orthodox Samaritanism for them, although since the 14th century orthodox Samaritanism has been enriched by the adoption of views which were formerly considered to be heretical and sectarian. Even if these latter views are considered today (by the priests) to be completely orthodox, then we as outsiders cannot express an opinion against this interpretation. The priests who instruct the faithful do not consider them to be fundamentally important. Be that as it may, the authors of such views were mainly forgotten or defamed; but if their importance prevented such a treatment, then their views would simply be considered as pertinent to existence.

There are three basic works of Samaritan historiography. Two of them were originated by priests; the third was not.

The first work which originated at the suggestion of the priests is called the Tolidah or "Chain of priests from Adam to the present". This work was published in the last century by Adolph Neubauer on the basis of a manuscript in the Bodleian Library.[27] In 1953 I published a lithographic edition of it in a limited edition which was based on the original text found in the house of the high priest at Nablus, which I photocopied in 1950.[28] This was a [p.18] more original text than Neubauer's text which contained much later marginal notes.

The Tolidah combined the genealogy of the high priests with statements of their tenures of office. Occasionally, however, events during their tenures of office are also referred to. One appendix gives an introduction to the Samaritan calendar. The list of high priests serves more than chronological purposes. Again and again the number of the years of Jubilees and the years since the creation or the possession of the land is mentioned. The age which the Tolidah gives to the antediluvian patriarchs, as Charles observed in the foreword to his edition of the Book of Jubilees,[29] is in striking agreement with what is stated in that book.

The older part of the Tolidah was written in the 12th century by Eleazar ben ʿAmram; but the present original text in Nablus was written by Jacob ben Ishmael, who was a priest in the 14th century. The author of the 14th century version of the Tolidah claimed to have copied this work without making any changes from a work which originated from the 12th century. Since then every high priest has added something to it. A sect ruled by priests, such as the Samaritans, whose priesthood was contested from the beginning of the Samaritan schism (if not earlier) would most probably have written its priestly genealogies with the greatest care. Therefore it cannot be assumed that Eleazar's Tolidah was the first Samaritan list of this kind. The genealogy of the high priests of Jerusalem in the lineage of the Zadokites in I Chronicles shows an amazing similarity to the corresponding part of the Tolidah.[30] Even Zadok himself appears in the Samaritan list. Eli from the family of Ithamar is a black sheep to the Samaritans--as the ancestor of the Abiatharites--as well as to the Zadokites of Jerusalem. Most probably the question here is not that of a late borrowing; this came rather with the priest from Jerusalem who brought the Mosaic Law to Shechem. This priest was probably none other than the son-in-law of Sanballat and the grandson of the Zadokite high priest of Jerusalem.[31] Here we can see that the Jewish priestly family tradition has influenced the Samaritans.

In other respects, the Exile at the time of Nebuchadnezzar[32] is the first exile for the Tolidah. [p.19] The destruction of the Northern Kingdom is not mentioned. The Tolidah certainly knows about the heresiarch Dustis,[33] but it is satisfied with barely mentioning him. It also mentions Hadrian[34] but says hardly anything about his conflict with the Samaritans. A more important entry is found in connection with Baba Rabba, a high priest of the 4th century.[35] Samaritanism had reached a low point at his time. It is said in the Tolidah that Baba drove the enemies of the Lord from the Land of Canaan and ruled as high priest for 40 years. He revealed the true religion, built a synagogue, taught the Torah, and organized schools. All the Israelites were returned to their home city (previously they had been uprooted by the Roman persecution). The priests were spread into the city of the Samaritans and also into other places. The Tolidah then offers a list of those who were sent by Baba to the different districts of Palestine. To every reference of a layman sent by Baba, it was added that a priest went with the layman. As we have already said, the Tolidah is essentially a list of the high priests, which may not be interesting to us. But such a list was very important for the Samaritans. They saw in it a confirmation that the covenant of Phinehas[36] had been handed down directly to the contemporary priests. Moreover, in its pre-Mosaic passages it showed that the men of the holy chain which began with Adam were the direct ancestors of the present-day priests. These priests claimed the merits, the blessings, and the covenant of their forefathers.

The _Samaritan Book of Joshua_ has been well-known ever since Joseph Scaliger obtained the Leyden manuscript of the work from the Egyptian Samaritans in 1584. The oldest part of the manuscript originates from the year 1362 and the most recent from 1513. In his 1848 Leyden edition,[37] Juynboll assumed that the present work was not written later than the 13th century, and he defended the uniformity of the work. This Arabic Leyden manuscript of the Joshua book claimed to be a translation from a Hebrew original, but scholars doubt that the Hebrew original ever existed. The present Hebrew text of the Samaritan Book of Joshua has been generally considered to be a retranslation of an Arabic text from the 19th century. This Samaritan-Hebrew Joshua slightly amplifies the biblical [p.20] report about the death of Joshua and Eleazar and ends with the remark that Phinehas, Eleazar's successor, wrote the calendar and the

Torah-roll of Abisha'.[38] On the other hand, the Arabic Joshua passes from the death of Phinehas[39] to a treatment of the disturbances which brought an end to the "Time of the Divine Favour".[40] This end was brought about not only by the fall of Eli of the lineage of Ithamar but also by the state of affairs in the family of Phinehas, the oldest priestly lineage, in which everything was not in order.[41] It is not only stressed that Uzzi had entered on the succession of the high priest Bukki, while Uzzi was still a minor and therefore lacked wisdom and experience, but we also find here, as well as elsewhere in the Samaritan-Arabic Joshua, a rather overt, critical attitude with respect to the priesthood as a whole. There are exceptions: Eleazar[42] and Phinehas[43] at the beginning of the report, and Akbun[44] and Baba[45] at the end. Now in the 4th century A.D., the high priest Baba Rabba was indeed a saviour of the Samaritan sect; but as we know from other sources, he was more like Joshua than like Eleazar, the famous ancestor of the Samaritan priests.

The Samaritan book of Joshua is therefore neither a priestly genealogy nor a chronicle. It is a haggadic Midrash like the Memar Marqah,[46] the Molad Moshe,[47] or even the Asatir.[48] The first half of the book of Joshua is a commentary on certain events in the Old Testament, e.g. the Balaam pericope; from the death of Moses and the designation of Joshua as the successor of Moses to the assumption of power by Joshua; the fulfillment of his mission; the conquest of the land and the distribution of the territory. It is probable that the original author of this section worked with an Aramaic Targum (perhaps Pseudo-Jonathan for the Pentateuchal reports and Targum Jonathan for Joshua) and not with some Hebrew text.

The many chapters which deal with the time after Joshua's death, with their late legends, are a great obstacle to the assumption that an independent tradition of the biblical book of Joshua underlies the Samaritan-Arabic Joshua. These [p.21] chapters are found in the Samaritan-Hebraic version of the work. However, even if the Samaritan-Hebrew Joshua was a work which is independent of the Samaritan-Arabic Joshua, that does not mean (in turn) that an independent tradition of the biblical book lies before us here. In the Samaritan-Hebrew Joshua we also find the remarkable legends of Shobach and Nabich,[49] even if it treats events--as in the older half of the Arabic Joshua--which are approximately parallel to the biblical Joshua.

We will no longer concern ourselves here with the Samaritan-Hebrew Joshua, but turn to the Samaritan-Arabic Joshua, whose existence is attested to in the 14th century and which belongs to the sources[50] used by the great Samaritan chronicler Abu'l Fatḥ. Scholarly interest in the Samaritan Joshua was concentrated earlier on the question whether the Samaritans once had a Hexateuch or whether they had an independent text of the book of Joshua which could be of value for textual criticism of the corresponding biblical book. In these discussions the most important question was neglected--what the compiler of the Samaritan Book of Joshua intended and what, in his eyes, Joshua signified for his time and generation. I maintain that the Samaritan-Arabic Joshua is a homogeneous work. As in the Scaliger Manuscript, legends were not added later to the work but are an integral part of the work. If the Hebrew text[51] which Gaster published were original, we naturally would confront a further problem. It could be that the Samaritan Joshua book fell into discredit by the partisan use of the biblical histories which had been inserted into the work. If this was the case, then the Samaritan parallels to the biblical Joshua book would have lost all their standing among the Samaritans, and later, since the so-called Samaritan Joshua-chronicle was accepted, practically every recollection of the biblical chapters as a separate work would have become extinct for a long time.

What was the purpose of the man who wrote the Samaritan Book of Joshua as we know it from the Arabic version? In my opinion the author was an opponent of the priests; at least he was opposed to the monopoly of the priestly party. But this monopoly was successfully questioned only in the time of Baba Rabba [p.22] in the 4th century A.D. We can[52] infer from the list of priests, the Tolidah, that significant events occurred during the high priesthood of Baba. He set up a synagogue[53] and schools and taught the people the Pentateuch; he also divided the country into districts and installed mainly laymen as their leaders.[54] It is possible that this was simply a new organization of the Samaritan community after a pẹriod of oppression by foreign rulers. That is the impression which the Tolidah would like to leave with us. But Baba's reform probably extended much further than what is touched upon briefly by the Tolidah. However, it is clearly parallel to what the Samaritan book of Joshua tells us about Joshua's influence. Is it possible that Baba was the new Joshua for the writer? But before we consider in detail an answer to this question of how the Samaritan-Arabic Joshua book presents the main heroes of the book, what the work reports about the last days of Moses should be shown briefly.[55] We hear that Moses entered the

Tabernacle to offer a sacrifice. He lifted the screen and scattered incense on the golden altar. He spoke to the people of Israel after he came out again and proclaimed to them that the "Time of Divine Favour" would come, as well as the time of wrath and misunderstanding. He told the children of Israel of the flood and of the Day of Vengeance and Recompense and told them the time of his return. Then he proclaimed to them the destiny of each tribe and that he would assemble them all in the last days. Finally, we are told that Moses, with Joshua and Eleazar, climbed up the mountain and that at nightfall a divine column of fire came down which separated their master from them so that no one knew what became of Moses. It is added that the lifetime which was measured out to him had reached its limit, the appointed time of his life with people had expired and he now deals directly with the Lord and His angels. Therefore Moses does not die but is taken up and will come again as the Ta'eb (Saviour). Until his return he remains with the angels.

Joshua, the disciple of Moses, was called the Mortal (one) and the Spiritual (one). After the death of Moses, Joshua received a direct revelation from God, and before the battle of Jericho he received a message from an angel.[56] Angels, so it is said in this work, watched over Israel at the first Passover. The heavenly hosts are [p.23] very real to the writer of this book.[57] The angel has Joshua give a copy of the Torah to the king of the two half-tribes [i.e. the king of Ephraim and Manasseh] and urge him to read it day and night. Thereby the angel lets Joshua inform the king that he could find wonderful advice in it on how to prolong life in this present transitory world and in the future world, and that it offered its reader protection from spirits, from the evil eye, disaster, witchcraft, and enemy treachery.[58] Joshua then built a synagogue on the top of the holy mountain, and the Tabernacle of the Lord was kept in it. According to this work, no one could see the Tabernacle except the Levite priests.[59] Joshua had precedence over the high priests. Although the priestly rights were retained, they were nevertheless restricted. Joshua spent one day each week with the high priest, another day with his leading laymen, and three days in continuous study of the Torah day and night.[60] He was also portrayed as a great conqueror. He and his lay leaders made possible the "Time of Divine Favour" through their wise administration. Even the priesthood had its duties, but they brought the "Time of Divine Disfavour" by their evil administration.[61] According to Samaritan tradition, this picture of Joshua is practically the only indictment against theocracy.

After the report about conditions under the priests Uzzi and Eli, who caused the light to be taken from the Tabernacle and darkness to be brought on,[62] our author hastens to the time of Nebuchadnezzar and the Exile.[63] Once again it is important to say that this is the first exile which the Samaritans recognize in the Tolidah. Therefore it is remarkable that the return is caused by circumstances which are reminiscent of the story of 2 Kings 17. While Israel receives orders from the king to return and rebuild the Temple on Mount Gerizim, the Jewish group on its own accord decides to build the temple in Jerusalem. In spite of fervent requests for unity, the Jews remain stubborn and the dispute probably had to be brought to the king for decision. Then the well-known quarrel between Sanballat and Zerubbabel follows with the trial by fire in which the Samaritan and Jewish versions of the Torah are thrown into a fire, in order to see which would remain intact.[64] Naturally Sanballat, the Samaritans, and their Torah are justified. The new temple is erected on Mount Gerizim [p.24], the altar service is once again resumed, and now the earth not only gives an ample harvest, whose absence had been the basis for the recalling of Israel from the exile, but the earlier "Time of Divine Favour" also appeared to have begun again as it was before Eli. In a typical manner this report shows us that in Samaritan historical writing the Jewish reports were simply transformed in order to form a basis for Samaritan polemic. Incidentally, this goes to show that in any case the schism was not caused by the Samaritans.

The next historical episode which will be dealt with is Alexander's visit to Shechem and the friendly treatment which he--as our author carefully emphasizes--bestows on the high priest and the Samaritans in general.[65] Once again Jewish legends serve as a basis for Samaritan history. From Alexander, the Samaritan Joshua book suddenly passes to Hadrian who has just besieged Jerusalem.[66] We do not need to deal here with how Hadrian found an image and an idol in the temple and how two Samaritans named Ephraim and Manasseh betrayed Jerusalem to the Romans.

More important is the reference to the Jewish assertion that the Samaritans destroyed by fire every place in which Hadrian had been. Later the Samaritans explained that this had not been addressed against Hadrian personally but belonged to their purification rites. The essential point in the story of Hadrian and perhaps the reason for its acceptance was the fact that in Hadrian's time, probably as a result of his persecution of the Samaritans, the Samaritan liturgies and the book of the high priest, with a genealogy which went back to Phinehas, were lost.

The Samaritan Joshua then turns to the time of the high priest Aḳbun, the grandfather of Baba Rabba.[67] On his deathbed Aḳbun prophesies that God would allow a man to rise from his son Nathanael who would gain the upperhand over the oppressors. This man would be Baba Rabba whose circumcision would be made possible with the help of the Christian bishop Germanus, although at that time all Samaritan religious rites were forbidden. The Joshua book ends--or rather it breaks off--with Baba's plan to destroy the brass bird which was set up by the Romans as a talisman on the summit of Mount Gerizim. It is said that when any Samaritan ventured out on the mountain, the bird betrayed him when it began to caw "Hebrew". In order to be able to destroy this bird, which was probably thought to symbolize Roman power, Baba got the people to approve the sending of his nephew Levi to Constantinople, where he would pretend to prepare himself for priestly office.[68] [p.25] As soon as he had acquired a high priestly rank, he would return and destroy the brass bird. Levi becomes a real archbishop and decides to visit the church on Mount Gerizim. The Samaritans hear of the impending visit of an archbishop, but they did not know that he is the nephew of their high priest; here the Leyden manuscript of the Samaritan Joshua breaks off. This may be enough to characterize the so-called Joshua Chronicle.

The third basic work of Samaritan history, the <u>Annals of Abu'l Fatḥ</u> from the year 1335, has used the priestly genealogy of the Tolidah and the Samaritan Arabic Joshua as its main sources. Possibly the copy of the Samaritan Joshua that was available to Abu'l Fatḥ was more complete than the Leyden manuscript. In it the story of Archbishop Levi is completed--he returns and the brass bird cries "Hebrew" when he reaches the Mountain. Levi demands the destruction of the bird after he explains that the bird must have been mistaken. That night Levi joins his uncle Baba and the Samaritans, who were no longer repressed by the Roman Talisman, and they massacre the Romans. But this is only the first of Baba's victories. Incidentally, Abu'l Fatḥ tells the story of Baba, the Archbishop Levi, and the brass bird with a sceptical undertone; and only so that no one would assume that he does not know the story.[69] Abu'l Fatḥ also refers to the Samaritan Joshua book in other passages, for example, in the stories about Shobach and Nabich and in the Alexander legends, which he passes off as history. It would be nice if one could explain the questioning of the story of Baba and the bird by Abu'l Fatḥ's critical acumen, but he probably doubts it for other reasons. Elsewhere whenever he uses the Joshua book as a source, he delivers the report as his own. In this context, however, he emphasizes that he is quoting an old Hebrew chronicle. Clearly he would not like to be responsible for its authenticity.

Abu'l Fatḥ was authorized in the 14th century by the high priest Phineas to write an official history of the Samaritans. The writing which underlies this work is the official priestly genealogy, the Tolidah. He admits in the foreword that a larger genealogical work was at his disposal which did not agree with the Tolidah and which he disregarded, apparently on the advice of his patron. However, he made use of the Samaritan Book of Joshua for all the time periods included in it. Clearly he has suppressed some things. Thus, for example, the transfiguration of Moses is not mentioned by him. [p.26]

Abu'l Fatḥ gives more information about Baba than the Samaritan Joshua. It is indeed possible that the Samaritan Joshua also contained more sections about Baba besides the story of the brass bird; but the reports which go beyond it in Abu'l Fatḥ could also have been from other sources. Even in the form in which it lies before us, the Samaritan Book of Joshua leads up to Baba, who is a kind of new Joshua. In one section of Abu'l Fatḥ's Annals about the work of Baba, we find that the parallel to Joshua is shown even more clearly.[70] This section could very well have been quoted from the Samaritan Book of Joshua. According to him, Baba was not only a great military leader, but he also put the house of religion into order again. The Samaritan Book of Joshua speaks of the loss of the Samaritan liturgies and priestly genealogies in Hadrian's time.[71] According to Abu'l Fatḥ's report, Baba found that the priestly genealogies were lost or irregular. He then got rid of the priests except for those who escaped from his control.[72] The Tolidah says nothing about this but only says[73] that Baba divided the land among lay leaders who of course had priestly companions. Abu'l Fatḥ's source further reports that Baba set up a council of wise men in Nablus of whom only a few were priests.[74] This body had its own house of teaching and a Mikweh directly next to the synagogue, which Baba had erected on the foundation of Joshua's synagogue on Mount Gerizim. The regional districts were assigned to these wise men for the supervision of matters concerning religion and questions of life or death. One hears nothing about the priests who were assigned to these learned laymen. The Tolidah had mentioned that Baba built a synagogue, taught the Torah, and organized schools. It does not tell us where he built this synagogue;

we learn that from Abu'l Fatḥ. It also reminds us of Joshua's synagogue which stood over the Tabernacle and enclosed it. It could be that Baba built the first Samaritan synagogue. Perhaps much of what the Samaritan Book of Joshua says about Joshua is supposed to be a justification of Baba's deeds. When, for example, Abu'l Fatḥ's source reports that Baba allowed the common people to study the law book, the Samaritan Book of Joshua also reports that Joshua attached importance to laymen reading the book. Abu'l Fatḥ or his source adds that all those except for the Sabuʿai had followed Baba.[75] These Sabuʿai, who were Samaritans, had their own synagogues and priests.

The supporters of Baba were the opponents of the Sabuʿai, and Baba was opposed to the priestly parties. Even Abu'l Fatḥ does not consider Baba to be a real high priest, as [p.27] Cowley has pointed out.[76] One further point is not mentioned by Cowley. The high priest Nathanael, Baba's father, appears to have been alive when Baba went to Constantinople for good. Also according to Abu'l Fatḥ, Baba was lured to Constantinople and held captive there. After his death Baba's son Levi went to Nablus, but died on the day of his arrival. The Tolidah does not mention Baba's son Levi at all. Even Abu'l Fatḥ does not describe Levi as a high priest, but for him the successor, Aḳbun, Baba's brother, is a high priest. On the other hand, the Samaritan Joshua says nothing about this son of Nathanael. All its hopes are put on Baba. According to the Tolidah, the heresiarch Dustis (Dositheus) appears in Aḳbun's reign. Abu'l Fatḥ also reports that Dusis[77] appeared during the high priesthood of Aḳbun and that he led Levi the nephew of the high priest astray.[78] In this passage Abu'l Fatḥ's Annals are very confused. It is entirely possible that this Levi, although here he is called the son of Phineas, Akbun's brother, was either Baba's nephew--the one who was sent by Baba to Constantinople--or Baba's own son. Baba was opposed to the priestly parties, and perhaps we do not go too far if we equate the Sabu'ai with the orthodox priestly parties. (By the way, the statement in Epiphanius that the Sabuaeans celebrated the Passover in Tishri, the 7th month,[79] out of animosity against the Jews is no argument against the conjecture which was expressed above. Juynboll traced their name back to the Hebrew shebu'a and agrees with the explanation of Epiphanius. But although the Sabuaeans may have had their own calendar, I think, however, that Epiphanius was wrong and that the name--which probably had something to do with the number seven--is, instead, connected with the seven festivals which the Samaritans who were ruled by priests in later times still had to observe strictly.) To be sure, the orthodox hierarchy, except for the suggestion which was mentioned by Abu'l Fath, never use this designation of the sect themselves. But they put great store in being the true Israel, the priestly heirs of the covenant with Phinehas. Thereby they admit that their claim may be disputed by outsiders, even though they did not allow any one of their own party to question it.

The chief opponents of orthodox Samaritans were the Dositheans.[80] Actually the Dosithean heresy lasted at least from the 1st century A.D. down to the [p.28] 13th or 14th century A.D. Abu'l Fath states that the Dustan heretical group may have appeared at the end of the Persian period. That is obviously false since the Jewish kings of that time were named as Simon and Arkia (Hyrcanus). We have every reason to assume that the Dustan sect and the Dusis sect were one and the same.[81] Just because the Tolidah mentions that Dusis appears in the reign of the high priest after Baba, Abu'l Faṭh inserted his long digression about the Dusis sect right in this passage. But the reference to the Jewish kings, Simon and Arkia, shows that the Dosithean heresy could have originated entirely in the Seleucid period. It probably had many branches, but clearly they all have common features about which we will have more to say later.

Here it may be enough to say that in the Jewish, Christian, and Muslim sources which deal with the Samaritans,[82] we have more or less strong traces of two kinds of Samaritanism and references to their teaching.

In the Midrash Tanḥuma is the Jewish account of the Samaritan priests Dostai and Sabbai who were sent out in order to teach the alleged Kuthites and other immigrants who were squeezed into the territory of the defeated Northern Israel.[83] This shows at least that for the Jews of the time when the Midrash Tanḥuma was put together the names of Dosithean and Sabuaean were so characteristic of Samaritanism that two earlier teachers with these names had to be invented. Even in Josephus, Theodosius (Dositheus) and Sabbeus were characterized as protagonists of the Samaritans in their showdown with the Jews before Ptolemy Philometor.[84] The Dosithean sect is also mentioned as an opposition party which struggled against the rest of the Samaritans in Egypt in the early 7th century A.D.[85] Even the Arabic authors Masudi (died 956) and Shahrastani (died 1153) knew about the deep schism in the Samaritans, of whom the Dositheans were a sect. In the 10th century of our era there was a Dosithean synagogue in Nablus which was destroyed and then rebuilt.

The overcoming of the schism in the 14th century is connected, I assume, with the fact that the Samaritan community or communities in Nablus were greatly diminished because the crusaders had brought much suffering to them. The high priest Phineas seized the opportunity to heal the centuries old schism. [p.29] First of all he saw to it that a satisfactory priestly genealogy, the Tolidah, was drawn up. That strengthened the position of the priests. Then Phineas commissioned Abu'l Fatḥ to write his Samaritan Annals with the help of the Samaritan Book of Joshua. This Book of Joshua had once been a justification of the Dositheans for the work of Baba Rabba, in whose time at the latest the Dositheans gained supremacy. Baba was too important a figure to have been omitted from Samaritan history. Therefore the Tolidah made him a respectable high priest. However, Abu'l Fatḥ indeed admitted that he had been a great man, but reported his defeat, and actually excluded him from the high priesthood. Thus Abu'l Fatḥ let stand the Dosithean picture of the Joshua book of his time; but at the same time he points out that thereafter not everything that Baba had done agreed with the ideal of a "Time of Divine Favour". In this way Baba was reinstated and what the Dosithean party had said about Joshua and the history which came after him was claimed with appropriate caution to be a part of the great unified tradition of Samaritanism.

CHAPTER II

"The Religion of the Samaritans" [p.30]

According to a widespread conception, Samaritan religion consists of the observance of the Torah in its Samaritan version and the reverence of Mount Gerizim as a holy place on which each year the Samaritans celebrated their Passover. On the basis of the story which is reported in 2 Kings 17, the impression has still been maintained that Samaritanism was substantially influenced by pagan elements which were integrated within it, even though in a modified form. Since Christians are so "Zionist", it seems completely absurd to them that the Samaritans consider Gerizim as God's chosen place and not Zion. For the Christian faith, to be sure, chosen places in general belong to the past, as Jesus advised the Samaritan woman in Sychar.[1] But if Christians had to choose between Gerizim and Zion as places of pilgrimage, they would certainly choose Zion because salvation has come from the Jews[2] and not from the Samaritans. In light of this position, it is meaningless whether Gerizim or Zion was once the chosen place, and indeed for the author of Deuteronomy Gerizim was the true chosen place;[3] since this work received its earliest form in the last days of the Northern Kingdom before it was found and finally edited under King Josiah of Judah.[4] In addition, Jerusalem has become just as holy for Christians as for the Jews because our Saviour was a Jew and not a Samaritan, and he "was crucified for us" in Jerusalem. Nevertheless, Samaritanism is also indebted to the Jews for many things such as their entire Pentateuch and priesthood.[5] If one wants to calculate correctly the amount of influence, then one must not overlook the fact that the schism between the Jews and Samaritans did not mean that all contacts between them ceased. Discontented members probably went back and forth between both religious communities for a long time and from time to time supplied something of the spiritual possessions of their community to the other side.

If we ask for a brief summary of the principles of the Samaritan [p.31] religion, then we find it in the confession which is in the personal prayer which accompanies their bodily purification before public prayer. This begins at an altar with the impressive phrase "at the gates of your grace"[6] and changes into a liturgical version of their confession of faith. There are many altars on Mount Gerizim.[7] According to the biblical commandment to appear three times a year "before the Lord"--as it appears in the Masoretic Text, or (as the case may be) "before the ark" as it appears in the Samaritan text[8]--three pilgrimages a year were made to Gerizim by the Samaritans. The aforementioned prayer was spoken at each of these altars at the beginning of the divine service. But we will come back to that;[9] it will only be mentioned at this point.

The Samaritan confession of faith includes five points:

1. Belief in the one God.
2. Belief in Moses.
3. Belief in the holy Law.
4. Belief in Mount Gerizim.
5. Belief in the Day of Vengeance and Recompense.

The liturgical version of their confession of faith[10] says nothing about the resurrection, the appearance of the Saviour, or a man like Moses. However these points appear as extensions of the five points in the form of the confession of faith which is used in their personal prayer. Therefore there can scarcely be any doubt that this liturgical form is very old. Even the Samaritan woman at the well of Sychar expected the Ta'eb or the messiah, as the author of John's gospel says. Moreover, Deut. 18:18 was quoted as a kind of postscript to the tenth commandment of the Samaritans. This commandment was derived from Deut. 27:1-4 in which "Gerizim" was read in the Samaritan Text (in place of "Ebal" in the Masoretic Text).[11] This classification of Gerizim as the chosen place with the coming of one who is "like Moses" is as old as the official text of the Samaritan Pentateuch. In this connection, it is very interesting that the woman in John 4:29, in her discourse with Jesus after she had emphasized that Gerizim was the place where her Fathers had worshipped God, raised the question whether Jesus was the promised messiah or not.

[p.32] Samaritan religion stressed the importance of faith more strongly than the Jewish religion. Perhaps a formal Samaritan confession of faith became necessary simply in order to be able to distinguish the Samaritans from the Jews. Then we would have in this distinction further evidence of the non-conformist spirit which filled this sect. Here the difference vis-a-vis Judaism is vast. To be sure one could also define the Jewish Shema' (Deut. 6:4ff.) as a confession of faith, but in any case it is only a very rudimentary symbol of faith. Rabbinic Judaism demanded belief in one God and also in the resurrection of the dead. But above all it demanded the observance of the 613 commandments and prohibitions of the Torah as they understood them from the rabbinate and put them together in the

Mishnah and the Talmud. Pharisaic Judaism described its concern as the honest attempt to produce a system of behavior appropriate to the Torah which would take every possible situation into consideration; and for this reason life, with its claims to scrupulous fulfillment of the commandments by the pious, became more complicated than at the time that the Torah was written down. Then after the Temple was destroyed and the priesthood was robbed of their function of divine service, study (i.e., intensive intellectual work) was restricted to specific commandments. So one managed with the rule: To study the Law is to fulfill it; and if one applied this concept to, for example, the sacrificial laws, one would dedicate himself to the task of developing them systematically. On the other hand, there was no interest in a Jewish systematic or dogmatic theology in the truest sense of the word, and there is still none today.[12] The Talmud included both halakah, i.e. valid teaching on practical questions, as well as haggadah, i.e. opinions on ethical and dogmatic problems substantiated by certain passages of holy scripture. On the other hand, Samaritans emphasized the significance of faith--both what the individual points of its confession of faith referred to as well as concerning what is mentioned in the Memar Marqah, a haggadic Midrash on the Law with special reference to Moses.[13] A Samaritan once said to me: "We are not like the Jews who do not believe the haggadah [p.33], but we literally believe everything that Marqah has said in his Memar." Up to this day, Samaritanism has attempted to observe the 613 commandments of the written law without any modifications. The Jewish rabbinate indeed expanded the scope of the Law, but it has always known that the Law was made for man and has tempered the Law's harshness as much as possible. The Samaritans did not do that. I have spent many Sabbaths with Samaritans and participated in their prayers and meals. We drank cold water and ate cold fish in order to satisfy the commandment that forbids the use of fire on the Sabbath (Ex. 35:3). Samaritanism is therefore stricter than Judaism. But at the same time it is less burdensome. The reason for this is that the Samaritan, if he has fulfilled the Law to the letter, does not let himself be bothered with it further in his daily life, such as by trying to hallow the whole daily routine or by constantly making himself conscious of the fact that he is a Samaritan, and that has unremitting consequences for his conduct. On the other hand, he submits himself spiritually to the control of the Law. Besides the confession of faith, Samaritanism at all times recognized a rather comprehensive systematic theological teaching which must be learned in all circumstances. Such an emphasis on orthodoxy as opposed to mere orthopraxis naturally opens the door to excommunication and indeed not only by non-observance of the official halakah, but also by criticism of the official conviction.

So in essence Judaism presents itself as an intellectual Lay-democracy. But until today Samaritanism has remained a priestly theocracy, which has always successfully opposed the formation of a learned and a self-responsible laity. In other words, Samaritanism has remained at the stage where Judaism stood when the Zadokite priests ruled in Jerusalem (hence about the time of Jesus Sirach ca. 200 B.C., before the Pharisaic movement became the trend after the departure of the old Zadokite family about 180 B.C.[14]). After the Jerusalem temple was recaptured, cleansed, and in use again, one must not forget that the Hasmonaeans did not re-appoint the old high priest Onias IV. The Pharisees had not come to terms at all with the legitimate priesthood, but they probably did come to terms with the Hasmonaeans and others whose claim upon the office of the high priest was poorly founded. But the Samaritan high priestly family, which was Zadokite, could maintain that it was a genuine priesthood from the tribe of Aaron. The continuity of the high priesthood was therefore a chief weapon of Samaritanism against Judaism. Here was [p.34] something which neither the Samaritans nor the Jews could ignore. In any case, it was the Samaritan priests from the tribe of Zadok who brought the Law to Shechem. It was received under their influence, and they saw to it that it remained in their hands. That is not to say that the Samaritans never tried to wrench power from the priests; but under the circumstances, it was nevertheless possible that those who attempted to do that were charged with having a propensity towards Judaism--simply because the priesthood was <u>the</u> trump card of Samaritanism against Judaism.

We do not know when the authority of the Samaritan priests in Shechem was questioned for the first time. But there are indications that it happened about 120 B.C. when John Hyrcanus destroyed the temple on Mount Gerizim. Later at the time of the Christian Roman persecution, Baba succeeded in transferring a part of the power which was in the hands of the priests to the laity. After the crusades, the high priest Phineas was even prepared for the sake of unity to annex the Dosithean sect to orthodox Samaritanism and to recognize some of their remaining literature as a legitimate part of Samaritan literature. With regard to its antiquity, we continue to grope about in the dark. The Samaritan Tolidah Chronicle assumes a period of 260 years for the "Time of Divine Favour".[15] But what is the point of time from which we must begin? A few years ago Abram Spiro suggested[16] that if we calculate 260 years backwards from the point of time of the destruction of the Samaritan temple by John Hyrcanus, then one arrives at 388 B.C. as an entirely possible date for the construction of the Samaritan temple on Mount Gerizim. Thus Spiro considered the 260 "years of divine favour" to be the time in which the Samaritans possessed a temple, and he thought they had projected this back into the time of Moses since they had no ancient history of their own. If this hypothesis is correct, then the Samaritans did nothing fundamentally different from the Jews who, during the Exile and afterwards, utilized their meager reminiscences of Aaron and Moses to create a historical basis for their own conceptions of the priesthood and sacrifice. In fact the Samaritan Book of Joshua appears to consider the time period from Sanballat to Hyrcanus and the time period from Sinai to Eli to be almost equivalent--at least insofar as it has to do with proofs of divine favour.[17] In any case, it is not clear whether the Samaritan Book of Joshua assumed the time [p.35] of Sanballat to be a return to the "Time of Divine Favour" after the "Time of Divine Disfavour" had temporarily come to an end. According to the official view, this lasted from Eli up to the present. But the chronology of the Samaritan Book of Joshua is hardly official. In connection with the destruction of their temple at the time of Hyrcanus and to the end of the period in which the Samaritans were politically superior to the Jews, the priestly supremacy had been exposed to attacks which came from the community itself as well as from outsiders. From an 11th century collection of Samaritan customs, the Kafi of Yusuf b. Salama,[18] we learn that there were Samaritans who did not consider it necessary to make a pilgrimage to the mountain three times a year since there was no longer a temple on Mount Gerizim.[19] In a characteristic way, however, it was stressed that the pilgrimage depended on the presence of the altars and not on the temple as such. At any rate, Abraham and Jacob had made a pilgrimage to Gerizim before a temple was there. The biblical commandment naturally formed the reason for the pilgrimage. But a second essential argument for the necessity of the pilgrimage was also stated. They needed the blessing of the high priest, and this could be given only three times a year and only on Mount Gerizim.[20] Now the Samaritan Bible certainly commands them to appear three times a year before the ark. This proved to be a serious difficulty since the ark had been hidden since the time of Eli. The solution was found in that the high priest still existed. So it was explained that the commandment would also be fulfilled by appearing on the summit of the mountain before the high priest. It may be that that is to be understood as the priestly argument which has always been used since the days of John Hyrcanus. Finally, there was also the argument that [p.36] no complete prayer could be performed without an altar.[21] For did Jacob not say: "This is the door of heaven" when he built his Mazzeba?[22] But altars were there as has already been said.

The divine pilgrimage services are very old. While the pilgrims climbed the mountain, Deut. 27 and 28 were recited antiphonically and so it is even today. Immediately after leaving the synagogue, collections of texts are read from the Law which have as a theme the renewal of the covenant. After

Deuteronomy is read, they visit the different altars.[23] At each altar a divine service is held like the Sabbath morning prayers in the synagogue.

I assumed for a long time that these divine services were a later addition to the pilgrimage routine. But now I realize that it is more likely the other way round since the whole divine service takes place only at an altar on the mountain, while the preliminary prayer is shortened in the synagogue, and the blessing is not bestowed in as much as no priest is present. In this connection it is perhaps significant that even the Tolidah with its official priestly genealogy states that Baba built a synagogue, opened schools, and taught the people the Law.[24] Therefore the Samaritans first received a synagogue in the 4th century A.D. It is also informative that we are told in detail in a comprehensive passage from the Samaritan Book of Joshua (which Abu'l Fatḥ quoted[25] about Baba) which parts of the divine service Baba wanted to entrust to the laity. Samaritan laymen in Holon in Israel still direct the service in this way today because no priest from Nablus can or wants to come to them.

Dositheanism was successful in the lifetime of Baba, but its beginnings probably go back to the time of John Hyrcanus. Therefore it needed about 400 years in order to prevail in Nablus. After Baba's death Dositheanism lost its supremacy; however it remained a power in Nablus. Although its fundamental principles, which were directed towards secularization, did not prevail, the reunited Samaritanism of the 14th century took over its speculations and its gnostic interests. Thus Samaritanism developed a creative energy which it had not experienced since the time of Marqah, who wrote at Baba's command. Dositheanism was the catalyst which set this reaction in motion. As was mentioned before, the great questioning of the priesthood began with the destruction of the temple [p.37] in the time of Hyrcanus. Abu'l Fatḥ tells of a Jewish heretic who came to Shechem at the end of the Persian period and founded a schismatic group which was called the Dustan sect (i.e. in Farsi, Friends).[26] But here Abu'l Fatḥ inadvertently or intentionally goes astray; while this story in his Annals agrees directly with the history of the Persian era, he names Irqana (Hyrcanus) as the Jewish king of that time.

Abu'l Fatḥ inserts an additional section about the Samaritan sects in connection with his long digression about Baba. He probably does this because the Tolidah mentions that Dustis appeared about this time in Nablus.[27] Now most of the Samaritan sects were only modifications of the Dosithean sect. That is even admitted by Abu'l Fatḥ's source. His report about the original Dusis (i.e. Dosithean) sect, which occurs in connection with all these sects, places it closer to the above mentioned Dustan sect than to the various sects with which it is supposedly related. Therefore it is not necessary to assume the existence of two different Dosithean sects only because Abu'l Fatḥ gives accounts of this sect in two different passages of his history.[28]

Dusis--as the heresiarch is called in the second report of Abu'l Fatḥ[29]--is a [p.38] heretic from Jerusalem. When he comes to Shechem (Nablus), he meets Yahdu, an ascetic Samaritan priest who no longer eats meat since the first-born (animal) is no longer being sacrificed. Since one no longer sacrifices, Dusis suggests to him that logically one is neither allowed to eat bread nor drink wine. Yahdu agrees, and he and Dusis agree to fast. However, Dusis does an evil deed and gives Yahdu's name to a prostitute, who comes to Yahdu on the Day of Atonement and insults him in the presence of the priests. Dusis disappears in the ensuing scandal. The only clear thing in this matter is that the destruction of the Samaritan temple is presupposed.[30]

After Dusis had left Nablus, he went to Anbata and lived with a widow named Amantu. There he wrote books, and before his departure he urged her to show them to no one who had not taken a ritual bath. Then he withdrew into a cave, fasted to death, and his corpse was eaten by dogs.[31] The high priest in Shechem sent his son Levi to find Dusis and hand him over for judgment. Levi and his friends went to Amantu's house, where it was explained to them that they could see Dusis' writings only after they had purified themselves. Then they went one after another into the Mikweh and said as they came out: "I believe in you God, and in your servant Dusis" (instead of "...in your servant Moses"). Levi scolded his companions; but after he had been immersed, he made the same confession. He and his friends agreed to conceal this fact. But on the following Passover, Levi introduced new readings into the Torah and confessed that he had received them from Dusis' work. Then Levi died as a martyr, but the sect lived on.[32]

If my assumption is correct that the Jewish dissident, Dusis, came to Shechem at the time of John Hyrcanus, then this story would explain why Josephus (in the 1st century A.D.) knew of a Theodosius who was a Samaritan leader in an earlier era.[33] To be sure, he puts him in the 3rd century B.C.; but from his statement we can only infer with certainty that in the

1st century either Dositheus or his sect was one of the two great figures which represented the Samaritans to outsiders. If I am correct, then for this reason it would also be clear why a Jew like Dositheus came at just that time [p.39] to Shechem. Moreover it will become even clearer in the treatment of the basic ideas of the Dusis sect. As everyone knows, the Hasidim supported the Hasmonaeans only in the initial phase of the Maccabean revolt. Abu'l Fatḥ mentions in his report about the three sects of the Jews--Sadducees, Pharisees and Hasidim--that the latter were also Samaritans.[34] By this statement either he only wanted to imply that they lived among the Samaritans or in their vicinity, or there was really a Samaritan sect of the Hasidim. Here it should be remembered that since the time of the Zadokite manifesto (Ezek. 40-48), if not earlier (cf. Ezek. 37:16, 19; Jer. 31:9, 18, 20), there was hope for a reconciliation of the North and the South, i.e., the descendants of Joseph and the tribes of Judah. Salvation, however, was expected from the Jews. Ezekiel predicted the appearance of a priestly messiah from the lineage of the Zadokites and a lay-messiah from the lineage of David. We do not need to discuss the significance of the Davidic messiah here. At any rate, Ezek. 40-48 had a far-reaching impression on the Samaritan as well as the Zadokite sects of Damascus and Qumran. We must remember that the Samaritans also had a Zadokite priesthood. At the time of John Hyrcanus, they were the only Zadokite priesthood which possessed a temple, if one disregards the followers of Onias IV in Leontopolis in Egypt. The whole Samaritan doctrine of the Ta'eb (Saviour) is patterned after Ezekiel's hope for a <u>Nasi</u>,[35] except that the Ta'eb is naturally not a descendant of David but is one who is like Moses. By the way, Deut. 18:18 was also used as a messianic verse by the Zadokites in Damascus and Qumran.[36] According to the Samaritan conception, the Ta'eb will find the lost vessels and the incense-altar of the Tabernacle again. With the correct tools the real Samaritan Zadokite priests will then do penance for Israel just like Ezekiel's Zadokite priests, and the "Time of Divine Favour" will return, just as the Shekinah (i.e. the "Glory of the Lord") will return to Ezekiel's new temple (Ezek. 43:4; 44:4), wherever that may be.[37] Works like Tobit, Judith, and 4th Ezra in the Apocrypha and Pseudepigrapha stress, on the one hand, that salvation comes from the Jews; while, on the other hand, they attempt to bring the Samaritans and Jews together in many ways. There were also people in Judah who were deeply interested in the division of Israel.[38] On the other hand, the Pharisees considered only themselves to be the true [p.40] Israel; even Jews with another viewpoint, like the Sadducees and the members of the <u>'Am ha'arez</u>, were excluded from the true Israel by them.[39]

Earlier we spoke of the Samaritan confession of faith in a prayer which one did not speak in the synagogue but only at an altar on the holy mountain. The prayer probably goes back to the time when the temple still stood on Mount Gerizim. The resurrection and the Saviour [i.e. the Ta'eb] are not mentioned in it.[40] Except for alleged references in the Torah, they are first found in the Marqah which probably belonged to the 4th century Dositheans. As far as the Torah is concerned, the teaching of the resurrection is based on the Samaritan version of the curse on Adam, "dust to your dust"; a passage which simply reads "dust" in the Masoretic Text. The conception of the Ta'eb is based on Deut. 18:18. Only in the hymns of Abisha' ben Phineas

(14th century),[41] which are still used today on the Day of Atonement, do we find both these teachings of the eschaton together. It was Phineas who reunited the Dositheans with the Samaritan lineage of the Patriarchs which was governed by the priests. A section of the hymn deals with the star of the Saviour who is born, lives, and dies in order to liberate Israel. The Divine Favour, whose way he prepares, remains for a time but not to the end--it is only an episode. This is the original conception. The other picture of the Saviour which we find in the didactic teaching of Phineas, agrees with that of Marqah. According to him, the Saviour does not appear until the end of time.[42]

An essential characteristic, if not actually the decisive moment of the self-understanding of Samaritanism, lies in the conception of a priestly religion founded on the Pentateuch which has its focus on Gerizim, just as early post-exilic Judaism had its focus on Zion. Even today only the priests can perform the circumcisions, conduct the weddings, compose the marriage vows (the Ketuḇah), pronounce someone ceremonially pure, and determine the calendar. That can be taken a step further. If one examines the little that is known about the differences between Sadducees and Pharisees, then one will find among others the questions of purity [p.41] and of the calendar.[43] The calendar was naturally important because of the festival days. For that reason if one wanted to create one's own sect in the Hebrew domain, one would first change the calendar. The appointed times of the festivals were of great significance for the validity of religious actions. Therefore until today the Samaritan priests issue a calendar twice a year for the following six months on the Sabbaths of Ẓimmut (15th Shebat for Ẓimmut Pesaḥ and 15th Ab for Ẓimmut Sukkoṯ). The Samaritan believer must have such a calendar, otherwise he would not know whether his Sabbath--or festival--prayer would be rendered worthless by performing it at the wrong time. Leviticus 23:2 places much importance on this point: "The festivals of the Lord, which you should announce, these are the festivals of the Lord," and we must add no others. The Samaritans celebrate seven festivals: 1. The Passover; 2. The Festival of Unleavened Bread; 3. The Feast of Weeks (Pentecost); 4. The Day of Sounding the Trumpets which is called a New Year only on each seventh year; 5. The Day of Atonement; 6. The Feast of Tabernacles; 7. The Harvest Thanksgiving Festival (Festival of Ingathering). The Festival of Unleavened Bread lasts seven days just like the Feast of Tabernacles. Pilgrimages to the summit of Mount Gerizim are made on the seventh day of the Festival of Unleavened Bread, at Pentecost, and on the first day of the Feast of the Tabernacles. Even Passover is celebrated on Mount Gerizim. The Kafi point out that the festival year begins and ends on the same summit.[44]

The contrast between the Sadducees and Pharisees, which is found in Judaism in reference to calendar and purity questions, can also be found in some way in the formation of the sects among the Samaritans. Therefore it is necessary to examine the sects of the Samaritans in detail. The Arabic sources Masudi and Shahrastani know only two sects which are important--the Dustan sect and the Ḳushtan sect.[45] In an earlier period we hear in Josephus of Theodosius and Sabbeus and in the Tanḥuma of Dostai and Sabbai.[46] Therefore there were only two basic sects, one of which was always connected with the name Dositheus. Now one will not go too far wrong if he assumes that the other sects, most of which were named "Sabbai", represented the priestly party, which was wiped out during Baba's reign but later came into power again. The [p.42] name "Sabbai" is reminiscent of the number "seven" (<u>sheba'</u>). Perhaps the orthodox priestly Samaritans were so named because they adhered precisely to no more, but also no less, than seven festivals. In this way the many differences which existed between them and the Dusis sects could have been expressed in a single word by this name.[47] A few of the Dosithean sects wanted to abolish the festivals completely, a few wanted to change the calendar, and a few even wanted to end the pilgrimage to Mount Gerizim. Yusuf b. Salama admitted that there was a time in which the opposition within the community was so great that the priests had to permit the laity to take turns in groups in worship by sacrifice, because the burden of sacrifices was too great for the individual.[48] Naturally that signified a serious threat to the position and influence of the priests. But if the celebration of the seven festivals, in a state of ceremonial purity, at a time which was prescribed by the priests, and with the required offerings, could be maintained, then this served at the same time to preserve the power of the priests over the laity.

If one studies the Samaritan liturgy of today, one will be very much impressed by two different things--by the very consistency of the whole which sometimes produces an almost monotonous effect and by an overwhelming consciousness of sin. The grace of God, His compassion, and His goodness are also stressed. But all this is not of much value to outsiders like ourselves but only of value to the Samaritans. The outsider, to be sure, finds a deep spirituality here, but warmth is absent in their services. That is connected with the fact that their service goes back again and again to the past reminding God of His covenant and of the merits of the patriarchs. In Judaism one also remembers the merits of the patriarchs; but after the destruction of the temple, the Tannaitic Rabbis turned against too strong an emphasis upon them, and no doubt not without a side-glance at the Samaritans--for there (among the Samaritans) the merits of the patriarchs, like everything else, were provided to the believers by the priests. Likewise the Samaritan emphasis on ritual purity exceeded anything that rabbinic Judaism possessed.[49] In all this Samaritanism itself bears the image of its priesthood.

[p.43] But Samaritanism made use of more than this. The real mystery of the sect came not from the priests but from the Dusis sectarians. But as we will see, these sectarians were not only occupied with questions of faith but stood in opposition above all to the priesthood. Like the Pharisees, they wanted to possess a part of the priestly power without becoming priests; and for that reason they could not afford to push aside as meaningless questions concerning purity and the calendar.

Even though they appear in Abu'l Fatḥ's Annals in widely separated sections, as already noted, we must consider the two reports about the Dustan sect and about Dusis to be two variants of the same thing.[50] As Abu'l Fatḥ presents it, the relationship between the teaching of Dustan and that of Dusis is comparable to the relationship between the Damascus Document and the Manual of Discipline of the Dead Sea Scrolls, i.e. the report about Dustan is more halaḵic, but both exhibit common characteristics and one gets the impression that both reports complement one another. According to one report, the Dustan sect disposed of the festivals and probably also the Samaritan priestly calendar too, for Abu'l Fatḥ reports that Pentecost was celebrated fifty days after the morning of Passover just as the Jews celebrated it. The Dustan sect further dispensed with the use of astronomical tables for the calculation of the calendar and alloted thirty days to each month. They probably had no access to the priestly calendar secrets which were always carefully guarded.[51] They set great store in hallowing the Sabbath correctly. Therefore they ate and drank on the Sabbath only from earthenware vessels, in order not to be tempted to clean the dishes used on the Sabbath, as would have been necessary with soiled metal vessels. Cattle of course would neither be fed nor watered on the Sabbath itself. A way was found to feed and water the cattle beforehand so that it lasted through the Sabbath.

The Dustan sect possessed their own priesthood and synagogues. Their halaḵah dealt with precisely the same things with which the priests were concerned, e.g. with questions of personal purity and the calendar, and with questions of ritual sacrifices, such as of the Kashrut. As far as the question of purity was concerned, [p.44] for example, they considered a well into which dead vermin had fallen to be unclean. As far as the calculation of the time of the monthly impurity of women was concerned, they modified it to the extent that the impurity did not begin until sunset. They also considered certain animals to be unclean after they were dead. They also explained that anyone on whom the shadow of a gravestone had fallen was unclean for seven days. These views of purity were still being contested in the 11th century by Yusuf b. Salama.[52] But the Dustan sect also believed that a priest could enter an unclean house and nevertheless could leave still clean, provided that he had not spoken in it. The purity of a house, which was adjacent to a house which had become unclean, was made dependent upon whether a clean or an unclean bird perched on it.

The eating of eggs which were found inside of dead birds was strictly forbidden, with the exception of eggs found in ritually slaughtered birds. This too was discussed in the 11th century.[53] Although the Dustan sect strictly observed their religious obligations, they were opposed to fasting and mortification of the flesh. But that opposition may be connected with their abolition of the festivals and specifically refer to Yom Kippur. [p.45]

The Dustan sectarians were opposed to saying: "Hallowed be our God <u>forever</u>!" They would probably hold, like the Rabbis in the Mishnah tractate Berakot, that one should say "to all eternity"[54] in order to show belief in another life. They were also opposed to common people pronouncing the Tetragrammaton and demanded that "Elohim" (God) should be said instead. It is interesting that only they, and not the priestly party, were opposed to that. That is also significant in reference to what we know of the Samaritan phylacteries, by which one bound oneself to the <u>Shem ha-Mephorash</u>, the strong name of God.[55]

In the report about Dusis, it is stated that his followers abolished all the festival days except for the Sabbath. They did not go from house to house on Sabbath days; and if they were in doubt about the appointed date of the Sabbath, they observed a day which they considered to be a Sabbath--not once taking their hands from their sleeves.[56] The followers of Dusis did not speak the Tetragrammaton but said "Elohim" instead.

It is reported that they cut their hair, probably in opposition to the Samaritan priests who as a general rule did not cut their hair.[57] The followers of Dusis also believed that a corpse would rise from the dead soon, namely just after burial, and would enter into paradise. Hence when a follower of Dusis died a belt would be put on him. They also put a staff in his [p.46] hands and sandals on his feet to be in complete agreement with the slogan: "When we rise from the grave, we want to be prepared."

Certainly all this shows that the Dositheans set great store in keeping the Sabbath and the purity laws. To be sure, the festivals were abolished, and changes were also made in the calendar. In addition, the name of God was surrounded with secrecy, and they believed in a life after death. Finally, in the report about the Dustan sect, one finds an obscure indication about references in books of the children of Moses[58] that God had been served somewhere else before he was worshipped on Mount Gerizim. The Adler Chronicle, a late work compiled at the end of the 19th century, asserts in reference to the books of Dusis that they were merely a Jewish version of the Torah.[59] On the whole, it can scarcely be doubted that the Dusis sect had priestly aspirations to a certain degree and that Jewish influences made an observable impression on it. Certainly this sect was not the Rabbinic Judaism of the Mishnah, but probably a Judaism like the kind of Judaism of the Hasidim and Essenes.

Abu'l Fatḥ mentions eight more sects.[60] The Adler Chronicle names seven sects and identifies them explicitly as varieties of the Dusis sect. Six of them are also mentioned by Abu'l Fatḥ. For his part, Abu'l Fatḥ names only one sect which is not included in the list of the Adler Chronicle, but this one appears to be identical with one of the sects which was already mentioned by him.

According to the Adler Chronicle, the first branch of the Dusis sect was the Ab'unai (the Ba'unai in Abu'l Fatḥ). According to Abu'l Fatḥ's report, they appear to have been connected with Jewish Christians and with Simon Magus. In any case, they were influenced by the Dositheans and had a center in Basan.[61] In addition, he explicitly establishes that they attempted to abolish the festivals. The Saduqai, which the Adler Chronicle calls the Zadduqim,[62] are also mentioned by Abu'l Fatḥ and are closely connected with the Ba'unai which is the first branch of the Dusis sect. They were convinced that the world would last because Dusis had died a shameful death and that Levi, the proto-martyr of the Dositheans, was stoned because Dusis and all the righteous of this world had died. They further believed that the winged dragon would rule all creatures up to the day of the resurrection. The Saduqai or Zadduqim bound their members to strict silence in order to prevent the secrecy of their ways from being betrayed to anyone else. Its center was in Maluf. Abu'l Fatḥ mentions that this [p.47] sect existed only seven years and that it was destroyed, because its secret teaching became known to outsiders and its meeting house had collapsed upon them.

The second major Dusis sect which is mentioned by the Adler Chronicle is called Abia and was designated by Abu'l Fatḥ as Abia and Dusa. Its leader was Anthami. This sect was more numerous than the Ab'unai. They had 120 members, and they believed that not all the commandments had been annulled, although Dusis had opened the door to the spirit of contradiction when he threw out the festival laws. The Abia people left Nablus on a Sabbath, crossed the Jordan, and went, as they believed Dusis had commanded them, into the wilderness and died there.[63]

The Kiltai (according to Abu'l Faṭh) or the Katitai (according to the Adler Chronicle) constituted the third Dusis sect. They are also supposed to go back to the Ba'unai. Their hostility to the Law is explicitly stressed. When they ascended Mount Gerizim they spoke before God: "O God, we want to do here what your prophet Dusis said. We have abolished all the commandments, and you are the only one who can reveal the Tabernacle." When they descended the mountain, they "barked" like dogs. Thereby "to bark" probably refers to "to prophesy" in a kind of word play which is similar to the way it was used by Paul in 1 Cor. 13:2.

According to Abu'l Faṭh[64] the fourth Dusis sect was the Shalya b. Tairun b. Nin or rather according to the Adler Chronicle the Sakta bin Tabrin ben Nin. They were few in number. However in contrast to the other sects, Abu'l Faṭh reports in great detail about it. Its heresiarch appears to have been of Jewish origin according to Abu'l Faṭh's presentation. When Shalya came to the Samaritans, he is supposed to have promised to reveal the Tabernacle,[65] and that indicates he asserted a Samaritan messianic claim.[66] Shalya insisted on asceticism, especially sexual abstinence. The early Dusis sect had palm leaves which had allegedly been dipped in Levi's blood and which were considered to be relics; and they believed that one could see the manuscripts of Levi only after a seven-day fast--and that one should pray submerged in water.

Shalya clearly changed the festivals under the influence of the Ba'unai and their criticism of this part of the teaching of Dusis which he had stood for earlier. [p.48] He interpreted Mount Gerizim as only a substitute for the eternal mountain and challenged the value of a prayer which was addressed to Mount

Gerizim since it was like a prayer addressed to a grave. He began to differentiate between a permissible marriage with female gentiles and contact with a woman during her monthly period, because a gentile woman does not make a man unclean. He strictly limited the rules about impurity of corpses in that he confined it to the first day and even that only when a real contact had taken place. He apparently insisted on vegetarianism, although he did not consider animals to be unclean. He explained, however, that a child may be unclean to the same extent that his mother becomes unclean by giving birth. Since it was obviously his view that in the present situation holiness was impossible, he lightened many of the commandments which dealt with ritual purity, and among other things he forbade too frequent ritual immersions.[67]

Shalya clearly turned against Dosithean customs, which are otherwise referred to, so that we receive from him indirectly a better insight into Dosithean purity laws. But the customs which he turned against are not very different from that which appeared in the 11th century in the Kafi of Yusuf ben Salama as a legal orthodox Samaritan priestly custom. Therefore in questions of purity, Dusis and his followers, except for the pronounced hostility towards the Law of some sectarian branches, differed very little from the orthodox priestly kernel of the Samaritans. Earlier the Dositheans were even stricter. As far as their attitude towards Mount Gerizim was concerned, Dusis and the Dusis sects were generally critical. Shalya probably put an end to the ascent of the mountain on festivals and pilgrimages. Abu'l Faṭh states that he followed Dusis in his views towards Gerizim. Like Dusis, Shalya no longer pronounced the Tetragrammaton and instead said "blessed is he".[68] He reorganized a few parts of the synagogue services and allowed women to participate together with the men in the synagogue service. He also arranged that for reading and prayer, the head must be covered; and therefore he commanded a Tallit to be worn. Prayer was performed while sitting and not while standing. Shalya called his soul the "authority" and claimed himself to be the Father of all. His disciples are supposed to be "the friends", and by their prayers to God, his spirit is supposed to be freed. They also prayed that he would not die on a Sabbath.[69] [p.49]

The fifth Dusis sect was, according to Abu'l Fatḥ,[70] the sons of Yozadoq, or the Sons of Zadok according to the Adler Chronicle. Abu'l Fatḥ said that they were the five brothers of Taira Luza. Zadok the Great of Beit Far'a was brought into connection with them. They are different from Shalya and his disciples in that they considered Mount Gerizim and the temple on it to be holy, and they kept the commandments and prohibitions of the Law. They insisted that corpses--even without being touched--made one unclean and that everyone who came close to a corpse must be cleansed on the first day by a bath. Shalya prescribed this only if the corpse had been touched. Although this sect differed from Shalya on these points, they nevertheless called him the "authority".

Abu'l Fatḥ says that they, like Shalya and Dusis, no longer said "Blessed is his name forever".[71] All Sabbaths were considered to be especially holy, and Abu'l Fatḥ appears to suggest that they also followed Shalya in this, although he mentions this attitude towards the Sabbath explicitly only for the followers of Dusis. According to him, the Sons of Yozadoq stopped saying, "Moses dictated the law to us" (Deut. 33:4), which is still a common refrain today in the Samaritan liturgy. Abu'l Faṭh also informs us that Yozadoq (or Zadok) moved to Alexandria and lived there with his followers and that he promised them divine grace on the condition that men and women would live separately from one another.[72] Bustunus then attacked the sect by sea with the result that many perished. However, no matter what blows of fate they might suffer, the survivors believed that they remained under divine grace.

The Adler Chronicle mentions two other Dusis sects. The first, named Alia, does not appear in Abu'l Faṭh, and even the Adler Chronicle says only that they lived in Alexandria. So there remains the Faskutai which is the last sect of the Dositheans that is mentioned. They denied the existence of paradise and the resurrection. Life was an affliction for them, and the only comfort was the sexual life. After they had indulged in copulation until they were satiated, they emasculated themselves in the conviction that their purity would be restored again in this way.

Thus the Dusis sect was split up into many smaller sects. For this reason, it is not surprising that the references to the Dositheans by the Church Fathers were often contradictory.[73] Dositheanism directed itself mainly against Gerizim and against the traditional priestly privileges, since these privileges were advantageous to the priests on festival days. By contesting the sanctity of Mount Gerizim, [p.50] abolishing the festival days, and altering the calendar, the Dosithean sects undermined the official teaching and thereby did precisely what Jewish messengers from the South may have hoped to do. Also by changing the purity laws, the authority of the ruling priestly group was put in question. In addition, the Dositheans believed in a future life and had a mystical teaching. Finally, they appear to have organized the synagogue cultus. But on almost all these points, the various Dosithean sects differed even more widely from one another with regard to the importance which they ascribed to them. Clearly Dositheanism has been influenced by Jewish sectarian sources. It is just as clear that Samaritanism is indebted to the Dositheans for the belief in the resurrection, as well as the gnostic and theosophical elements which one encounters in Samaritanism after the annexation of Dositheanism to mainstream Samaritanism. If one studies the Samaritan Pentateuch or the Samaritan Targum, one finds no signs of a belief in angels; and even the idea of the "Angel of the Lord" is explained away.[74] In the Samaritan Targum, there is no Memra-teaching[75] and even no haggadic material. The Pentateuch and Targum are [p.51] the official documents of Samaritan priestly orthodoxy. However the Memar Marqah, which is based upon the Targum, also contains Dositheean teachings. Therefore we find clear doctrinal statements in it with regard to the angels and the pre-existence of Moses and his ascension.[76] In the Memar Marqah, Joshua is also a king. The fact that the haggadah of Marqah has become a part of orthodox Samaritanism shows that Samaritanism was enriched by Dositheanism. Nevertheless the teaching of the Memar Marqah still encountered stiff resistance in the 11th century. To be sure, Abu'l Hassan al-Suri devoted a section to the angels, but the angels are mentioned by him only in passing. He also mentions the death of Moses;[77] but in the Jewish Targum Pseudo-Jonathan, its haggadic development is even greater, while it is suppressed in comparison with Marqah.

Therefore about the 11th century A.D. the Dositheans were still a heretical sect.

The references to the Samaritan sects are sparce, but one can at least recognize what they opposed. If one studies Samaritanism today, then one can ascertain that much of what one considers as orthodox today was originally heretical long ago. So it is said in the Malef, a textbook for Samaritan children,[78] about God's word: "It became light!" This Light is the Holy Spirit, i.e. Moses. Adam and also Eve are clothed in this Light. Belial seduced Eve, and she in turn seduced Adam with the yetzer ha-raʿ. Then Man lost his body of light and received a fleshly body in return. However a spark of light remained in him, which will be further handed down until the incarnation of Moses, for whose sake the creation takes place. Adam was destined to die, but he was spared for the sake of Moses. Adam and Eve were expelled from the Garden which was guarded by the cherub of conduct (i.e. the halaḵah) as well as by the cherub of the Law (i.e. the Torah). Cain and Abel are the sons of Beliel. The children of Cain are the "children of the darkness". Adam knew Eve after a long period of being a Nazirite and produced Seth in the image of God. The holy chain of the "children of the Light" descended in the image of God from Seth, which led to Moses who brought the Law.[79] The Law changed all Samaritans (and only them) into potential "children of the Light". But they must be awakened, and the fleshly body which they have as a result of the sin of Adam must be judged. Then they will [p.52] ascend to the Garden of Eden since Moses intercedes for them. Even Jews and gentiles will be awakened, but since they do not belong to the chosen ones they are already condemned to hell.[80]

This is orthodox Samaritan teaching today, although I doubt they will report it as such to outsiders. It belongs to the secret teaching of the Samaritans even though it appears again and again in the Samaritan liturgy. The contacts with Qumran and Christianity are striking.[81] Nothing is found of that in the Samaritan Pentateuch and in the Samaritan Targum. But there was a Dosithean sect, the Saduqai, whose name alone would suggest a relationship with the Zadokites of Damascus or the Zadokites of the Dead Sea. The suggestion that a few of the Dosithean teachers were Essenes is not to be excluded. Finally, Epiphanius refers to the existence of a Samaritan Essene sect.[82]

CHAPTER III

"The Samaritans and the Gospel" [p.53]

In the time of the New Testament there were still many Samaritans in Palestine, probably even more Samaritans than Jews, and they represented a permanent challenge to Judaism. Moreover, both the Judaism as well as the Samaritanism of the first century were each split into different groups.

The Mishnah and the Talmud speak contradictorily about the Samaritans.[1] Many times the Samaritans are simply ignored and then attacked; sometimes they will even be praised, even though reluctantly. In addition to the Talmud there are several apocryphal books,[2] which are indeed convinced that salvation comes from the Jews, but which still attempt to heal the wounds of Israel's separation.[3] The gospel of John is directed to them.[4] On the other hand, the gospel of Matthew is opposed to the Samaritans. The Samaritan problem does not appear in Mark at all, but Luke realizes that the first mission of the church had to be made to Samaria before it could apply itself to the truly pagan world. Therefore I assume that there was not only [p.54] another kind of proclamation of the gospel vis-a-vis the Samaritans in Luke and in the book of Acts, than in the Fourth Gospel, but that this is addressed to another group among the Samaritans. If Judaism took the Samaritan problem seriously, it is all the more likely that the Christian church did so. And since the church believed that the gospel applied not only to the Jews, it is obvious that in the expansion of its missionary work it first turned itself to the Samaritans. They were not really considered to be pagans by the Jews and were even considered by many Jews to be true converts; but only a few writers considered them to be a true part of Israel.

It has been said that the gospel of Luke may have been written for gentiles. Then I wonder for what part of the gentile world it could have been destined. Luke reports in the book of Acts how the gospel first came to Samaria and was not proclaimed to real pagans until after the Apostolic Council of Jerusalem.[5] Even Peter was not opposed to the evangelization of Samaria.[6] Nevertheless according to Luke, Jesus called the Samaritan leper a "foreigner", an ἀλλογενής,[7]--with this word the exclusion of the heathen from the temple was explained. It is entirely possible that the early church did not lack voices which used the success of the mission to the Samaritans as proof for the world-wide relevance of the gospel. Indeed the Samaritans were similar and yet also dissimilar to the Jews. Therefore they had to be the test for how far the conservative group among the Apostles was prepared to go. Thus Peter was sent forth to examine the faith of the Samaritans for its authenticity. The result fully satisfied the church and this procedure became an important prerequisite in return, so that the works of Paul among the pagans would come to the "apostolic council" in order to be completely acknowledged.[8] However the debates over the expansion of the mission were only a temporary problem. The battle was already won when the gospel of Luke was written; and the gospel could be preached in Jerusalem, Samaria, and the whole world. But not all the Samaritans were won. For example, there were still the Dosithean Samaritans,[9] who certainly in the long run did not represent a very difficult assignment especially since the Dosithean heresy [p.55] was dependent on certain branches of Judaism. It was even more significant that the hardened nucleus of the Samaritan-priestly orthodoxy had remained, and that the author of the gospel of Luke and the book of Acts addressed himself to them. In general he stressed priestly concerns, and it may very well be that he knew the Samaritan priestly traditions and customs and attempted to show that Jesus might also be the fulfiller of the Law and its promises for the Samaritans.

In spite of much criticism, I still firmly maintain today the conclusions of my work which I wrote in my essay on the Samaritans and the Fourth Gospel[10] to which I will continuously refer in the following. To be sure I see that they consider only one aspect of Samaritanism. In the meanwhile I have obtained a more complete picture which now includes everything which I said in the last chapter, that the Samaritan schism was not only separated from Judaism, but was also itself split into different groups during the greatest part of its history. That Samaritanism, to which the gospel of John addressed itself about 100 A.D. and which is identified today with orthodox Samaritanism, was not yet orthodox in the 1st or 2nd century but existed in the form of the Dosithean heresy. Naturally the author of the gospel of John took care to point out that salvation comes from the Jews [Jn. 4:22]. From the point of view of the Samaritan Dosithean theology, much in the gospel of John would have been more attractive if Moses had been put in the place of Jesus. But nevertheless does it not make concessions to the Samaritans? Are there not good reasons for the Jews accusing Jesus of being a Samaritan [Jn. 8:48]? These facts compel me to discuss several statements in my essay which was mentioned above.

We will begin with the story of the woman at Jacob's well (John 4:1ff.)! Here it is clearly stated by Jesus himself that salvation comes from the Jews [p.56] (4:22). On the other hand, Jesus testifies to the Samaritan woman that he is the messiah (4:26). Although the Samaritan woman did not ask about a Jewish-Davidic messiah, the Jewish concept of the messiah is employed. Nevertheless Jesus is designated many times in the gospel of John as the prophet who is to come, and this is connected to an expectation which is based upon Deut. 18:18. The application of this passage with regard to the messiah cannot be based on the rabbinic writings. In turn, Deut. 18:18 is the basis for the Samaritan messianic or Ta'eb expectation. This is intended to throw some light on another connection. When John 7:40-43 tells of a quarrel among the people over whether Jesus is the prophet of Deut. 18:18 or whether he is the Davidic messiah, the question comes to mind who could have thought of the conjecture that he is this prophet? Were there perhaps Samaritans in the crowd whom Jesus had aroused? Gentiles would have scarcely asked these questions and the same must be true of the Greeks named in 12:20 who were obviously Greek Jews who had come to the festival at Jerusalem!

The first references to the messiahship of Jesus in the Fourth Gospel are shaped by the testimony of John the Baptist (1:15-36), from which Andrew's testimony to Peter (1:41) also originated, and by the confession of the Samaritan woman that Jesus is the salvation of the world (4:42). This Samaritan confession is emphasized by the Evangelist in that he has the Jews say that Jesus himself may be a Samaritan and have a devil (8:48). In three other cases (7:20; 8:52; 10:20) he has them say approximately the same thing. But he also has Jesus reject the charge that he has a devil, while he only has him ignore the statement that he may be a Samaritan. There can be no doubt that Jesus was not a Samaritan for John. But why then does he allow Jesus to remain silent to the accusation that he may be one?

In the great speech of the Good Shepherd (10:16) Jesus says he has other sheep who are not of this fold. By this the Jewish community is surely meant which should form, together with the "others" <u>one</u> herd with <u>one</u> shepherd. Clearly the Evangelist is thinking here of Ezek. 34:22-24: God will judge the sheep and his servant David will be his shepherd. But in Ezek. 37:15ff., the prophet is also ordered to take one stick and to mark it with "Judah" and a second stick with "Ephraim", and to tie both together as one stick to symbolize the reunification of Israel and Judah. Ezek. 37:24 comes back to this promise once again--David should be from Judah, and he will be the only shepherd of them all. No matter what time we ascribe Ezekiel's words to, the inhabitants of Northern Israel at his time were Samaritans. So it is possible that when Jesus speaks of other "sheep" besides the Jews, he is thinking of the Samaritans who, according to this gospel, are the only non-Jewish group whom he directly approached and the only ones who accepted him (cf. 4:40 with 1:11).

[p. 57] When Jesus answers the questions of the Samaritan woman, he points out to her that salvation comes from the Jews, but that he may also be the one who brings the fulfillment of Samaritan messianic hopes. He adds that the fields, by which he can only mean Samaria, are already "white for the harvest" so that his disciples would harvest there what the Jews have not sown (4:35ff.). However it is probably not without great significance that all this is mentioned so soon after the story of

Nicodemus (3:1ff.). While Nicodemus, as a Jew, cannot understand what Jesus means by the necessity of a rebirth by the Spirit, the Samaritan woman is deeply impressed when Jesus speaks of a time in which men will worship God neither on Mt. Gerizim nor in Jerusalem, but everywhere, that is in spirit and truth. Just as Jesus's words about the one shepherd and one flock take up Ezekiel's promises, and are indeed from a passage which is closely connected with thoughts of the reunification of Northern Israel with Judah; so in Jn. 3:5 Jesus's words to the "Ruler in Israel" of the necessity of a new birth by water and spirit likewise appear to be based on Ezekiel, namely on Ezek. 36:25f., where there is talk of sprinkling with clear water, of a new heart, and a new spirit. Certainly Jesus uses Ezekiel's thoughts here with an objective which far exceeds their original meaning; but in such a way that even here the view of the prophet is unmistakably felt which looks forward with ardent expectation to the reunification of divided Israel.

Therefore if it is true, on the one hand, that the author of John's gospel does not give up the Jewish statement that salvation comes from the Jews; and, on the other hand, that he wants to show that Jesus is the fulfillment of all the hopes of Israel (both the hopes of Judah and the hopes of the Samaritans, who are assumed to be the descendants of Northern Israel); then must we not certainly expect to find elements in the gospel of John which must appear so Samaritan to the Jews that Jesus would appear to be a Samaritan to them? The author of the gospel has intentionally not simply referred back to the corresponding statement; and indeed there is an element which agrees with the Samaritan faith, because he hoped to be able to show that in his version of the preaching of Jesus. Can one assume then that the author of John's gospel has attempted to build a bridge in Christ between Samaritans and Jews?

But what is in Jesus's message that could be put on the side of the teaching of the Samaritans? In order to be able to answer this question, it is necessary to take note of a few of the main points of Samaritan Theology.[11] This statement forms its basis: God created with ten words. In particular these words are: With the first [p.58] word, "Let there be light", God created "the light which was the Holy Spirit, which he allows to remain in the loins of the prophets, and which he manifested in the form of our Lord Moses in the invisible and visible world." This light, i.e. the Holy Spirit, is considered by the Samaritans to be the pre-existent Moses. Then the actual creation was done for Moses' sake, who is the highest of all the visible and invisible creatures, the source of all light. Adam is created on the sixth day. The angel of the Lord formed him from the dust of the earth, and God breathed in him the breath of Life. Adam was like us, but at the same time different from what we are now, for he was like the angels and had no evil impulse. Adam and Eve still had no sex in Eden, i.e. Eden was holy and sex is unclean. Adam and Eve were also clothed in light in the Garden. But the evil spirit Belial brought in the snake and seduced Eve. Adam listened to Eve because he received the evil impulse from her which she had received from Belial. So Adam ate the forbidden fruit. He would have died immediately if the image of Moses, the light of the first day, had not been concealed in him. "Look," God said, "Adam has become like one from him."[12] Since Adam and Eve then had to leave the Garden, their clothing of light was stripped from them. They received a clothing of skin; that is they received a fleshly body as the

Samaritans interpreted it, and the evil impulse was in the skin. The Samaritan Pentateuch reads in the curse laid on Adam in Gen. 3:19: "Your dust" instead of "Dust", i.e., "Dust you are and to your dust shall you return!" They hold the view that here the return of the spirit to the flesh is meant, namely to his own flesh; thereby spirit and flesh can be judged in the resurrection. After that, the spirit obtains a new body of light and enters paradise covered with light and is no longer covered with flesh. The ancient story then goes further: Eight days after they had left the Garden of Eden, Adam knew Eve. After that, Cain and his twin sister were born, then Abel and his twin sister. The descendants of Cain are the sons of Belial.[13] Therefore they are not created in the image of God, but simply in the image of the "Fallen". Not until after Abel was murdered by Cain did Adam repent his own sins before God. He repented for 100 years and during this time he kept a vow of sexual abstinence. After God [p.59] had forgiven him, he knew Eve again and Seth and the other children were born. God, who received Adam's repentance mercifully, thus created with him the pure lineage from which the prophet Moses came. All the rest of mankind, except for this pure branch which forms the Samaritans as the true Israel, are considered to be "fallen".

The Samaritans compare the two cherubim over the Ark of the Covenant with the two cherubim which are set up at the gates of Eden in order to guard the way to the tree of life. The Law is the tree of life in the sense of the eternal life. All who eat of its fruit are now already potential dwellers of paradise, since the Law is the true way to eternal life. After Adam had sinned, he and all his descendants were destined to receive the sentence of death. That was necessary because only in this way could he lose his fleshly body with its evil impulse and recover the body of light which had belonged to him before the Fall. After the resurrection, he will be a spiritual being clothed in light as he was originally. Moreover, it is especially noteworthy that men could not participate in eternal life until Moses, the Light of the World, brought the Law. But then and even now eternal life is only for the true Israel, which the Samaritans consider themselves to be.

If we now turn again to John, it is striking what emphasis he lays on "the Word". It is certainly to be admitted that in Samaritan theology there is no developed doctrine of the Logos. On the other hand, light is as important in Samaritan theology as in John. Again and again the evangelist refers to the light: "In him was life, and the life was the light of men" (1:4); John the Baptist "was not the light but he came to bear witness to the light" (1:8); "that was the true light which enlightens every man who comes into this world" (1:9). "It [i.e. the light] was in the world and the world was made through it, but the world knew it not" (1:10); "but as many as received him, to them he gave the power to become children of God" (1:12). Jesus's references to himself as the "light of the world" (cf. 8:12 and 9:5) and that those who believe in him will become "children of the light" are very important.

A comparison of Samaritan ideas with the thought of the gospel of John reveals the following common interests and differences: The pre-existent Christ in the gospel of John takes part in the creation, but one finds nothing about that among the Samaritans. Also it cannot be determined whether in Samaritanism it is the light of the first day (the Holy Spirit who is the pre-existent Moses) which participates in the work of creation. However, it is said that the light of Moses was the origin of the light of the stars and the spirit of the prophets, i.e., it was utilized in the creation [p.60] and was at work in men before Moses came in the flesh into the world. In John it is then said that the light "was the true light which enlightens every man who comes into this world" (1:9). According to the Samaritans, this light was in Adam and was inherited from him through "the prophets", i.e. the Patriarchs down to Moses. But it was not present in every man before Moses's appearance, but at most in a few Israelites. Even after Moses had revealed the Law, it was made accessible only to the Israelites and not to the gentiles. The light that God called into life with his word on the first day of creation was the Holy Spirit and at the same time the pre-existent Moses; but in John the Holy Spirit is the spirit of Jesus, and Jesus is the light. Therefore we still have the same identification of the Holy Spirit and light as in Samaritanism.

Looking back at the charge of the Jews that Jesus may be a Samaritan (8:48), it can be said that enough traits are found in the Johannine picture of Jesus to have suggested to the Jews that Jesus was in any case different from the Scribes and Pharisees, at least as far as we can get a picture of them based on the later rabbinic writings. The emphasis which he puts on faith instead of on the fulfillment of ritual religious acts must have made him appear strange in comparison with the former. If the speeches in 8:1ff. have real historical foundations, it cannot be surprising that "the Jews" looked upon Jesus as a Samaritan.

In this connection, it appears to me to be totally false if one interprets the question of the "Jews" to Jesus in 8:19: "Where is your Father?", as if they wanted to charge him with illegitimate birth. In 6:42 they have already said: "Is this not Jesus, Joseph's son, whose father and mother we know?" It is very prejudiced if one reads into the assertion that Jesus is a Samaritan a reference to his alleged illegitimate birth based on 2 Kings 17 in which the Samaritans are considered to be illegitimate Jews. Instead the Jews profess in 8:33 to be freeborn descendants of Abraham who do not need to be liberated, and they are not able to see that they are slaves, i.e., slaves of sin. As they emphasize once again that Abraham is their father (8:39-44), Jesus makes it clear to them that if they want to kill him they are not acting like Abraham but like Cain: "You do your Father's work." The answer of the "Jews"--"We are not born out of wedlock"--again is not thought to be a defamation of the virgin birth of Jesus, which should already be apparent in the second part of their statement: "We have a Father, God." Finally, therefore, it is not a question about Jesus but about the "Jews". Therefore in 8:44 Jesus says that his Jewish opponents are of the same species as their father the devil, as a result they could not accept the truth about which Jesus speaks. Now certainly for someone who was himself Jewish that was a very astonishing assertion about Jewish teachers, and for those to whom it applied it was simply impossible [p.61] that a Jew would say something to that effect about other Jews. But that was not enough! Here was someone working along the same lines as the Samaritans. If the old story of 2 K. 17:24f. which concerns the "Kuthim" and other settlers in the destroyed Northern Kingdom and which called the Samaritans a mongrel race, originated from the Jews, then their Samaritan opponents went even further and asserted that the Jews were no better than the gentiles, i.e. the descendants of Cain who inhabited the Land and married, in part, the descendants of Seth. Calling the Jews "sons of the devil" would not have been entirely unusual for a Samaritan. However if the "Jews" called Jesus a Samaritan because of such a statement, it may not be taken literally, for it is only a question of his behaving like a Samaritan in so far as he appears to take up a Samaritan polemic. In addition, it is true that even if the gospel of John were written in Ephesus, it would be a complete distortion to view the Samaritan-Jewish quarrel, as it stands in the background of John 8, merely as a local Palestinian matter, for there were Samaritans at that time throughout the empire. However, within the narrow compass of these explanations, the possibility can only be pointed out that the Fourth Gospel interprets Jesus's preaching in a way which would be more attractive to the Samaritans, and which even the Jews themselves must have considered to be friendly to the Samaritans.

In summary then what Samaritan theology ascribes to the pre-existent Moses, with respect to participation in the creation, the gospel of John ascribes to the pre-existent Christ. On the other hand, according to John, men will now be able to become sons of light, i.e. to be released from the burden of sinful flesh; for the Samaritans, that cannot happen until the day of the resurrection when Moses appears as the mediator. But of course this is true only for the Samaritans. Finally, the Law mediates eternal life to the Samaritans while eternal life comes to Christians through faith in Christ. Likewise just as Moses intercedes for the Samaritans now and at the end, so Christ does for his own. But this is done for Christians without respect to whether they come from Judaism or Samaritanism. What St. John had seen Jesus produce in his time (after Jesus' death and resurrection) by His spirit, the Spirit of God, is for John certainly bestowed upon the Samaritans and the Jews but also upon the whole world beyond Israel.

In contrast to the gospel of John, the gospel of Luke begins and ends with a reference to the temple.[14] Luke possesses sound knowledge about the temple [p.62] and about priestly concerns.[15] This is very surprising when one considers that Luke is very interested in the impact of the gospel on the gentile world. Naturally everything here depends upon what the word "gentile" means for Luke. It is of course important when Jesus called the Samaritan leper (the one who had been healed by him and who was the only one of ten lepers who thanked him) an ἀλλογενής, i.e. an alien. But the Samaritan villagers who rudely refused hospitality to Jesus and his disciples did not receive the punishment which was wished by the disciples. Instead the disciples themselves were scolded by Jesus because they had asked him to call down fire from heaven on the Samaritans.[16] The Parable of the Good Samaritan presents the Samaritans in a most favorable light for his conduct towards the badly abused Jew is more brotherly than that of his Jewish συγγενεῖς.[17] That the parable says this about a Samaritan allows his point to be made so much clearer. Indeed the Samaritan is no neighbor of the Jews from a Jewish-legalistic standpoint but an ἀλλογενής and outsider.[18]

The book of Acts, which also has the same author as the gospel of Luke, shows a clearly positive interest in the Samaritans. In Acts the mission to the Samaritans is the first step in the mission of the church to the gentiles. My thesis is that for the author of the gospel of Luke and the book of Acts, the Samaritans, who indeed do not belong to the rabbinic-Jewish community and who according to their own self-understanding do not belong to Israel, represent an essential part of the gentile world to which he wants to turn. If Luke had thought of the gentiles only in the customary sense, then he would have hardly [p.63] given so much space to information about priestly matters. He would have hardly mentioned the priestly order to which the father of John the Baptist belongs, the circumcision of Jesus on the eighth day, Mary's purification, and many other things.[19] One could object that Luke only wanted to show that at the same time that Jesus is the fulfillment of the Law, he fulfills it himself; and indeed he says in Luke that the Law was really in effect until the time of John the Baptist.[20] But even the Samaritans believed in the Law and kept it.

Let us pursue these things a little more closely! The Samaritans maintained that the Jews could not keep the Law at all either in the right way or even on the basis of the teachings of the Rabbis. Yusuf b. Salama's chief criticism of Judaism was that the Jews had forfeited the name Israel because they postponed circumcision until the eighth day.[21] He explains further that they had forfeited the right to be considered as heirs of the covenant because they had changed various purity laws. Finally, the Samaritans considered the Jewish priesthood to be illegitimate, because they were descended from Ithamar, the ancestor of Abiathar, through Eli.[22]

A few remarks need to be made here about the situation of the Jewish-Zadokite priesthood after the Exile. To be sure, they did not manage to gain complete control over the temple of

Jerusalem and its services, as the author of the Zadokite manifesto had hoped (Ezek. 40-48). Nevertheless up to about 180 B.C., they were in the majority and appointed the high priests. But this did not happen without compromise. In place of the Levitical priests, i.e. the sons of Zadok in the time between Joshua and Ezra of whom we hear about in the book of Ezekiel, two groups appear--on the one hand, the Zadokite priests and, on the other hand, the Abiatharite priests. Both are assumed to be descended from Aaron, the Zadokites through the older son Eleazar and the Abiatharites through the younger son Ithamar. Since all Aaronites could be priests, the Zadokites without a doubt had to recognize the Abiatharites as priests. But they saw to it that the majority of the priestly duties and the high priestly office were appointed by them alone.[23] Thus a new stabilization of the Zadokite preponderance was attained. This is shown by the fact that even after the true Zadokite lineage had lost the right to appoint the high priest in the middle of the second century B.C., the Zadokite order continued for ordinary Zadokite priests. Thus Zechariah's group or the Abijah group was Zadokite.[24] But the Samaritan priesthood [p.64] was entirely Zadokite. That naturally created a feeling of great superiority in Samaria.

Furthermore, we know that the Samaritans and the Sadducees frequently agreed on halakic questions, for example with regard to the date of Pentecost. This was probably not the only agreement in calendrical questions,[25] to say nothing of other agreements.

A difficulty is created in that we know very little about the views and customs of the Sadducees from the rabbinic-Jewish sources. Rabbinic Judaism came into power after the year 70 A.D.

and soon and determinedly began to supply itself with Sinaitic authority and to prove that its ideas had always existed.[26] The Mishnah and the Talmud are not primarily interested in history. Where they do make historical determinations, these appear only in order to bolster the claim of the Rabbis to the absolute credibility of their teachings.[27] Eighteen differences between the Pharisees and Sadducees are set forth in the rabbinic sources. The Sadducees play a roll therein which is unbecoming to them, and this is naturally done on purpose. Among these traditional differences, the calendrical and purity regulations were the most important. It was primarily in this respect that the Sadducees as priests had to oppose the Pharisees. While, in their view, the Pharisees were forced to snatch authority from the priests in these areas if they ever wanted to win complete domination in religious matters. So everything here is more or less pragmatic.

Perhaps the study of the Samaritans can now contribute to what our Jewish sources have depicted and help us to reconstruct a reliable picture of priestly and lay Judaism as it existed before 70 A.D. Indeed many scholars today are still of the opinion that it must be possible to test the accuracy or inaccuracy of certain New Testament statements about the Judaism of the first century, above all in reference to the Pharisees, by drawing inferences from rabbinic Judaism which did not even become decisive until after 70 A.D. Rabbinic Judaism did not immediately become "Normative Judaism". It was dynamic and not static. Surely many ideas and customs of rabbinic Judaism were not yet present in the Mishnaic period, [p.65] but were first taken up much later. Nevertheless, they were already willingly considered to be integral component parts of the official Judaism of the first century. Thus for example in the Acts of the Apostles, the concept of Pentecost, as the day on which the new Law of the Holy Spirit was given, is said to be a Christian reinterpretation of the Jewish-Pharisaic conception of Pentecost as the festival of the remembrance of the day of the giving of the Law upon Sinai, although there is no historical basis for this in the Rabbis. Similarly, the glossolalia, which is reported in the same connection, is still regarded here and there as a Christian reinterpretation of the Jewish haggadah according to which the Law was revealed in seventy languages, although there is no proof for the greater age of the haggadah. Such things are repeated with regard to our information about the differences between the Sadducees and the Pharisees. We know that they quarrelled over the date of Pentecost, but we hear nothing more about it. The Mishnah certainly says nothing about Pentecost as a festival of the giving of the Law. It contains no particular tractate about the festival of Pentecost at all. On the other hand, even today the Samaritans observe Pentecost as a harvest festival as well as a festival of the giving of the Law. So, too, the Book of Jubilees, which was well-known to the Samaritans and to the Qumran sect and which certainly did not originate from Pharisaic circles, considers Pentecost and the giving of the Law to be of great significance. It cannot be considered impossible that the Pharisees also connected Pentecost with the annual date of the giving of the Law--only we know nothing about this. However, it appears that rabbinic Judaism first accepted this interpretation much later when it no longer considered those sects to be rivals, who had first made use of Pentecost combined with the festival of the giving of the Law.

But let us return to Luke! We read in the gospel of Luke (1:5ff.) of the message of the angel to the priest Zechariah of the Abijah order, that his wife who until now had been barren would give birth to a son and that he, John, should be a Nazirite throughout his whole life. Since, as a priest, he was not permitted to cut his hair anyway[28] but could drink wine and strong drink; only the prohibition of the latter makes it clear that the child would be a Nazirite. Indeed it almost appears as if his being a Nazirite is more important to the narrative than his priestly descent. Now the Mishnah discusses the state of being a Nazirite in such a way as if, at the time of its redaction, it were a permanent institution. It tells[29] the story of a man who was a Nazirite for a year and afterwards [p.66] died, although according to the Mishnah the vow was supposed to last only about thirty days.[30] Further individual instructions are that the Nazirite must give a certain sacrifice at the end of his term,[31] and it is even considered to be a pious duty to help a Nazirite in the payment of his sacrifice.[32] As far as it goes, the Mishnah also reduces the possibility that a man could give up the Nazirite vow too hurriedly. On the other hand, the Samaritan codex of the Law of Yusuf b. Salama[33] characterizes the Nazirite as a man who consciously gives up not only the joys of the world, but also work and matches the holiness of the high priest.

Yusuf b. Salama speaks of Nazirites who live with one another like brothers and sisters. According to him, the difference between a Nazirite and a high priest consists, among other things, in the fact that the holiness of the Nazirite is only a fleeting thing, while that of the high priest lasts. A Nazirite must let his hair grow, but at the conclusion of being a Nazirite it can be cut again, while the high priest's hair is never cut. A Nazirite never drinks wine; while, on the other hand, the high priest occasionally drinks wine. One becomes a Nazirite if one has the desire, while a high priest is a high priest from his birth to the end of his life. Thus, as Yusuf explicitly emphasizes, a Nazirite is only partially like the cohen (or priests). All this clarifies the status of the son of Zechariah and Elizabeth in Luke, John was a Cohen. Although he was not a high priest, on the basis of his continuing Nazirite life he was just as holy as the high priest.

Yusuf, who wrote in the 11th century A.D. when the Samaritan high priesthood still existed (while the Jewish high priesthood had long since vanished), could say: "One can be a Nazirite in our time only as long as there is a high priest and water for purification."[34] He adds that no Jewish priest could be of use to a Nazirite in the fulfillment of his vow; only the Samaritan high priest would be able to do that because only his genealogy would be above all suspicion. According to Yusuf, it is not permitted to be a Nazirite less than 373 days, hence one solar year plus seven days of preparation which corresponds to the seven days of preparation of the high priesthood. The Naziritehood of John was most unusual for its kind in rabbinic circles. Although Samson (Judges 13:5) and Samuel (1 Sam. 1:11) were known in holy scripture [p.67] as Nazirites, the Rabbis were evidentally ill-disposed towards all exaggerated asceticism. What is the reason for that? Perhaps it is connected with a threat, like that which was felt to come from the Qumran community.

According to Luke 1:24, Elizabeth conceived her son (John the Baptist) fairly soon after the week of service of the Abijah order was completed. If we knew precisely at what time in the course of the year was Abijah's turn in the temple, we would at least know approximately when John the Baptist was born. Considering the condition of our sources, only certain rational speculations are possible. Let us assume that the year of service began at the same time as the festival year on Nisan 1,[35] then the week of the Abijah order would end two months later since it was the eighth in order, therefore about the end of Iyyar. John would then have been born at the end of Shebaṭ, the 11th month of the festival year. According to Luke 1:24, Elizabeth hid herself five months, and in the sixth month of her pregnancy the announcement of the angel came to Mary (1:26, 36). Therefore for Luke, this Annunciation appears to have happened at the beginning of the eighth month of the festival year, in Marheshwan. In any case, according to Luke, approximately six months lay between the birth of John and the birth of Jesus (1:36). If our assumption is correct that Abijah served in the spring; then, according to Luke, it would follow that the birth of John the Baptist should be put at the end of the Jewish festival year before Passover, the festival of liberation. Hence Jesus's birth should be placed one or more months before Sukkoṯ, the autumn festival.[36]

Only very few precise statements are possible at this point; still it may be possible that the author of the gospel of Luke, with his interests in priestly concerns, tried to make a certain symbolism apparent. John is born on Shebaṭ, and Jesus was born on Ab. Ab is supposed to have been an especially important month for the Jews, since the Temple and Jerusalem were destroyed on Ab 9; and to this very day this is a month of sorrow for them. It should not be forgotten that, in the ancient festival year of the Jews and Samaritans, the festivals lie in a period of six months from Nisan to Tisḥri. In the Pharisaic-Jewish festival year, Hannukah, the Festival of Lights, takes place as the occasion of remembering the rededication of the temple under the Maccabees and incidentally at the same time as the winter solstice. On the other hand, the Samaritans have two special Sabbaths respectively two months before the Passover festival and the Feast of Tabernacles. They are called the Sabbaths of Ẓimmut and fall respectively in Shebaṭ and in Ab--apparently therefore on the respective birthdays of John and Jesus (see above)--on the Sabbath before the full moon of these [p.68] months.[37] The Sabbath of Ẓimmut Pesaḥ is also called "the door to the festival time period". On the occasion of these two Sabbaths, the Samaritan high priest publishes the calendar for the following six months. But at the end of Shebaṭ and at the beginning of Adar, the Sabbath stands for Sheḳalim--a temple sacrifice.[38] The Jews have the New Year of the Trees on the 15th of Shebaṭ. Rabbi Gamliel speaks in M. Taʿan, IV, 10 of an earlier festival on the 16th of Ab which was connected with the ξυλοφωριά, the offering of wood for the altar. It may be that when the temple still stood, these Sabbaths were intended to be half-festival-days of preparation for the great festivals in Nisan and Tisḥri on which the priests informed the laity when the festivals were to take place. The Pharisees later added Purim on the 14th of Adar in order to be able to show in the story of Esther that God was able at all times to save Israel from the gentiles, as He had done in the time of the Egyptians.

It should not be assumed that the dates indicated by Luke and the interpretation which we gave to them supplies us with the real dates of the Annunciation or the birthdays of John and Jesus. As has already been said, Judaism was not really interested in dates per se, and the authors of the gospels were even less so. Even the Jewish haggadah is not a historical writing, not even where it takes up historical facts. It is enough for it, if it can elucidate a point of halakah by an "event".[39] In performing biblical studies, it is not enough to pit history and myth against one another as true and false. The authors of the New Testament, as well as the authors of the Old Testament, knew that the historical facts alone were not enough in order to make the truth evident, just as archaeology cannot supply proof for the assertions of the Bible. The gospels deal with historical facts, but they have the freedom to interpret them in order to make the spiritual inferences perfectly clear. If I am right with my assumption that the birthday of John the Baptist would suggest to the Samaritans that his birth was, so to speak, the opening of a door to the coming salvation; then that is to say, in other words, that for the ordinary reader John was the Elijah who was to come before the messiah Jesus.[40] If the birth of Jesus is really to be set[41] before the great festivals in the 7th month when the sabbatical year was announced on the 7th year, then the eyes of the Samaritan and perhaps also the Jewish reader would be opened with regard to his future significance. But that is not enough! Besides her personal thankfulness, is there not [p.69] in the Magnificat of Mary (Luke 1:46ff.) in her visit to Elizabeth--both women are pregnant--also an expression of the significance of the coming event for all of Israel? It is true after all that God has not forgotten his covenant! Ẓimmut is considered by the Samaritans as the day of the meeting of Moses and Aaron, when Moses had returned to Egypt in order to free his people. Therefore could it be that at the meeting between Elizabeth and Mary in which the child in Elizabeth's womb jumps (1:44), the reader is supposed to be reminded of the meeting between Aaron and Moses? Isn't John from a priestly family, and Jesus the new Moses? Let us not forget that in Luke's Acts of the Apostles (3:22; cf. 7:37) Jesus is the prophet who is to come. Or rather in the gospel of Luke and the Acts of the Apostles should we not be led to the fusion of the priestly and prophetic in Jesus himself?

David is not mentioned in the Magnificat but in the Benedictus Dominus (Lk. 1:68ff.). This agrees with the belief which would be fulfilled of a Zadokite priest, as Zechariah probably was, that "the Lord has raised up the horn of salvation in the house of his servant David".[42] John, the son of his old age, becomes a sign to him that God remembered the oath that he had sworn to Abraham, so he recognizes in his son the prophet who will proclaim the impending salvation. What is suggested to the Samaritans by the birth of John, in a season during which they were preparing for the coming festival of salvation, appears here to be said to the Jews in a way that they could also understand what is meant.

The song of praise of the angel in Luke 2:14 is likewise of great interest for our examination. In verse 9, the expression "Glory (<u>Kabod</u>) of the Lord" could recall the so-called angel of the Lord in Samaritan angelic lore;[43] but it is more likely that it is connected to the Shekinah, the divine presence, i.e. the presence of the Lord with men. In Ezekiel the Shekinah abandoned the first temple and then returned to God's new temple.[44] Now the Shekinah is present here with the shepherds.[45] (The Samaritans believed that it had been in the Tabernacle on Mount Gerizim, but it disappeared after Eli's schism.[46] The Shekinah was considered to be a sign of the grace of God; with its disappearance the time of mercy ended [p.70] and the time of disfavour began.) Even the motif of salvation which comes from the Jews appears to be emphasized. In the city of David the Saviour, Christ the Lord, is born, and the heavenly hosts proclaim the presence of the mercy of God. A Samaritan who read that could really find in that statement the fact that now the "Time of the Divine Favour" had begun.

Also a Samaritan must have asked what the emphasis on the circumcision of Jesus on the eighth day (2:21) meant. In addition, Luke explicitly emphasizes that the purification of Mother and child was fulfilled according to the Law of Moses. The "Nunc Dimittis" of old Simeon emphasizes beyond this the significance of Jesus for the gentiles as well as for Israel. If Simeon was the son of Hillel and the father of the elder Gamaliel, then it could be possible that Luke wanted to show that the best in Pharisaic Judaism had recognized the future significance of the child Jesus. His further recognition by Hannah from the family of Asher shows how very intent Luke is on emphasizing the universal recognition of Jesus. Finally let us not overlook the tale of the twelve year old Jesus (2:41ff.). Although Jesus grew up in Nazareth the temple in Jerusalem was his Father's house for him.

The year of the baptism of Jesus by John is indeed stated (3:21), however we know nothing about the precise date. To be sure, it may be inferred from the fact that Jesus spent forty days in the wilderness after his baptism (4:2) that these forty days are supposed to represent the forty years of the wandering of the people of Israel. In Samaritan and Jewish synagogues the wandering in the wilderness was remembered by special readings in the weeks between Easter and Pentecost. This is the case even today in the Samaritan liturgy.[47] The time between the two feasts is dedicated to fasting and meditation by Samaritans and Jews. Or was Jesus baptized when the crowd which had been at the paschal festival in Jerusalem was now returning home again? In any case, the emphasis on divine grace in the words of the voice from heaven in the baptism of Jesus (3:22) confirms the earlier remark in 2:52 that Jesus grew in the favour of God and Man. The Samaritan reader could not overlook this emphasis on the grace of God.

Even the genealogy of Jesus which goes as far back as Adam (3:23ff.) is important--not only because Jesus is descended from the father of all mankind, as it could be interpreted by the gentile, but above all because it could appear to the Samaritan priests that Jesus belonged to the holy seed; for the genealogy of the Samaritan priests likewise emanates from Adam.[48] In the Samaritan prayers and the Malef [p.71], the son of light is emphasized. According to John 8, Jesus is not a son of Belial like the sons of Cain. But his genealogy is also no priestly genealogy; Jesus is rather, like Ezekiel's *Nasi*,[49] a descendant of David. But even the Ta'eb, who is identical to Moses, was not expected to be a priest.[50]

The fact is significant that for Luke Jesus begins his spiritual activity in Galilee. It would be interesting if the haftarah from Isa. 61 had been read by him in Nazareth in the month of Tisḥri. Third Isaiah, as is reflected in his statement on the proclamation of salvation, had thought of the year of dispensation as "proclaiming the year of the Lord's favour" (Isa. 61:2; Luke 4:19). For a Jew, these verses from Isaiah signified that Jesus asserted a messianic claim. On the other hand, for a Samaritan, although the book of Isaiah was not recognized by them, these verses signified that he was the Ta'eb with whose coming the "Time of Divine Grace and of Favour (Raẓon)" would begin.

Later after Jesus had brought to life again the son of the widow of Nain (7:11ff.), the people said: "A great prophet has arisen among us and God has visited his people!" Here again it is not only emphasized that Jesus is a prophet but also that God has shown mercy on his people. Then in the following section John's disciples ask Jesus (7:19): "Are you the one who is to come or should we wait for another?" For the Jews, "the one who is to come" could be the Davidic messiah, but for the Samaritans, "the one who is to come" is the same as Moses. Perhaps Luke is intentionally unclear here. In the passage (20:41ff.; cf. Ps. 110:1) where Jesus proves to the Sadducees that the messiah cannot be called David's son--if he had been, David would not have called him "Lord"--perhaps Luke wants to emphasize not only the origin of the messiah, but also that one could overemphasize the doctrine of the Davidic sonship of the messiah. Therefore this may not be the best way to speak of the messiah, although it makes it more attractive for the Jews and especially for the Zadokites of Jerusalem.

The transfiguration of Jesus together with Moses and Elijah (9:28ff.) clearly shows that Jesus is the hope of the Jews and Samaritans, for the Jews consider Elijah [p.72] to be the forerunner of the messiah, while the Samaritans believed that the messiah (Ta'eb) would be one who is like Moses. Here Jesus has the approval of both of them, and Luke expects that Jesus will be accepted by the Jews and Samaritans.

Even the combination of the Parable of the Lost Sheep (15:1-7) with the Parable of the Lost Son (15:11-32) can be significant. The father of the lost son had two sons. Perhaps one represents Judah and the other Samaria?

At the conclusion of our work with the Lucan conception of a gentile world which includes the Samaritans, it is worthwhile to take a look at Stephen in Acts 7:2ff. It is remarkable that he is charged with blasphemy against Moses and against God. In his defense the accused pleads various things which could not have been taken from Jewish sources, as for example that Jacob and the patriarchs were buried in a tomb in Shechem, which Abraham had purchased with a sum of money from the sons of Hamor--the fathers of Shechem. According to the Jewish tradition, Jacob was not buried in Shechem. Abraham had bought no grave there, and only Joseph's bones were buried in Shechem.[51] Not even the Samaritan tradition speaks of Jacob being buried in Shechem. It is very strange that Stephen would stress Abraham's and Jacob's connection with Shechem in a defense before the high priest. Is it possible that the author of Acts wanted to show his sympathy for the Samaritan claim that Shechem was sacred to the patriarchs? With its summary of Israelite history, Stephen's speech, judging from its approach, could have originated from a Samaritan priestly source. By referring to the time of Moses and the Patriarchs, he could obtain a hearing and at the same time reject the charge of blasphemy against God and Moses. But in order for us to make things perfectly clear, we must look at the whole speech. To put it briefly, it is a survey of God's dealings with his people from the call of Abraham until the coming of Jesus.

More than half of this survey is devoted to the time from Abraham to Moses. Special importance is ascribed to the latter's words to the children of Israel (7:37): "A prophet will be raised up for you by the Lord your God from your brothers in the same way that he raised me up"; you should listen to him! Israel's faithlessness against God is emphatically set forth at the time of the wandering in the wilderness, and even the reprimand by Amos 5:25ff. is cited. But Amos's prophecy of disaster for Northern Israel was transferred to all of Israel including Judah, in that the quotation "beyond Damascus" is changed to "beyond Babylon" (7:43). In particular it is emphasized [p.73] that there would be only one true tabernacle of testimony established by God in the wilderness, and this true Tabernacle had come with Joshua into the country (7:45) where it remained until the time of David. David had found grace in God at that time and wanted to erect a Tabernacle for the god of Jacob, but Solomon had done it erroneously with respect to God, for it is said (7:48): "The Most High does not dwell in temples which are made with hands." Stephen expressed thereby that according to scripture the Shekinah had never been in the temple at Jerusalem. Therefore he considered Solomon's building of the temple to be a great offence and sees that the temple is precisely not the place that God would select for his glorification.

But Stephen also emphatically attacks the Jewish priesthood. He reproaches them for their fathers had persecuted and killed the prophets who had spoken of the coming of the Righteous One (7:52). They had also not kept the Law which had come to them through angels (7:53). The obvious temptation is to conclude that this reference to the giving of the Law by angels, as well as specifically to the angel who spoke to Moses on Mt. Sinai (7:38), and the appearance of the angel of the Lord in a burning bush (7:30) originates from the Jewish fear of anthropomorphism; and at the same time that one can recognize the influence of that idea in Jub. 1:27; 2:1 according to which an angel was the mediator of the Law. The high point of the speech, where Stephen says that he sees the Son of Man standing at the right hand of God (7:55), shows, however, that it was not fear of anthropomorphism which influenced him to mention the intervention of an angel in God's discussion with Moses. Much more is meant; the old has been disposed of and now there is direct access to God.[52]

As we have already seen, the gospel of Luke and the Acts of the Apostles occupy themselves with the temple a great deal. The apostles preached and the first Christians prayed in the temple. To be sure they appear to have done this not because it was the temple; but because, in a manner of speaking, they were carrying their battle into enemy territory. Except for the father of John the Baptist in the gospel of Luke and the priests which came to the faith in the book of Acts (6:7), the real enemies of Jesus or, as the case may be, of the apostles in Luke are the temple priests. That is a new tendency in Luke, but it is also new with him that he makes a distinction between the scribes and Pharisees in a way that is not done in Matthew.[53] In Luke, in contrast to Matthew, the Pharisees appear in a more favorable light than the priests, scribes, and the Sadducees, such as when Gamaliel in the Sanhedrin inhibits the threatened persecution of the [p.74] early community (Acts 5:34ff.) or when Paul claims to be a Pharisee and makes use of Pharisaic arguments against the Sadducees (23:6). No doubt Luke turns against the priests and temple because for him both belonged to the past and in the new order of the Spirit there is no longer a place for them. Anyway for him it is not simply the case that one must return to a relationship with God which was given with Moses and the Tabernacle, whose plan had been shown to Moses (7:44); for this was only an archetype of the future reality, just as Moses was a forerunner of the one who would come. The Samaritans, especially the members of the orthodox-priestly group, naturally agreed with every criticism of the Jerusalem temple and its priesthood; and that means that the Christian message, at least as it is reflected in Luke, could find an audience in their circles. Indeed they were looking for a redeemer who was supposed to be like Moses. Therefore it is also notable that Stephen does not maintain that Jesus is the Davidic messiah, and he does not mention Jerusalem a single time.[54]

After the case of Stephen, the book of Acts reports that as a result of the persecution of the community in Jerusalem all the faithful (except for the Apostles) were scattered into the countries of Judea and Samaria (8:1). For example, Philip went into "the city of Samaria" (Shechem?) and preached successfully about Jesus to the Samaritans (8:5ff.). Even Simon Magus, who was considered by the Samaritans to be "the great power of God", was deeply impressed because the unclean spirits were driven out of the possessed and the sick were healed, and he allowed himself to be baptized (8:9ff.). Thus he observed that the gift of the Holy Spirit, which was conferred by the Apostles through the laying of hands, gave to the receiver a greater power than that for which he had been famous up to that time. He had claimed that he was a "Great one" so that he could claim to be the Ta'eb, yet now Jesus was proclaimed to be the Ta'eb. Then Simon wanted to be reinstated, and he demanded that the Apostles transfer the full power of the Spirit to him. From other sources, we learn that Simon later claimed to be for the Samaritans what Jesus was for his own, the Jews.[55] The author of the book of Acts shows the direct dependence of Simon on the Apostles, for according to Luke's presentation the Spirit had not yet come by baptism to Simon or the other Samaritans.

Naturally this story also has a second aspect, as was suggested earlier. The results of the mission into Samaria were so unexpected that the Apostles went there in order to examine and possibly approve the work which had been done there. [p.75] In any case, it is significant that after his work among the non-Jewish Samaritans, Phillip continued his journey in order to convert the Ethiopian Eunuch who was scarcely a native Jew, even if he professed the Jewish religion (8:26ff.). However, the church was established in Samaria--just like the church in Judea and Galilee (cf. 9:31)--as a church of the circumcision, before the first gentile, Cornelius, was accepted by Peter (10:1ff.). The Samaritans had received the Holy Spirit as a confirmation of their previous baptism by the Apostles. However, a greater miracle had been necessary for the gentile Cornelius since he received the Holy Spirit without the laying on of hands. Thereupon Peter, who was instructed by a special vision, agreed to Cornelius' baptism (10:44ff.), and even then the brothers in Judea still demanded an explanation from Peter. The fundamental problem of whether the uncircumcised should be received in general was therefore still not solved at all by the reception of the Spirit by Cornelius who was uncircumcised and unbaptized.

The principal remained that "Unless you are circumcised according to the custom of Moses, you cannot be saved" (15:1).

Naturally some gentiles who were not Samaritans lived in Samaria. Perhaps these were the ones who were converted by Paul and Barnabas on the way to Jerusalem (cf. 15:3). Luke probably had only these gentiles in mind and not the gentiles as a whole. The Samaritans practiced circumcision and insisted that only one who had been circumcised on the eighth day, as Jesus had been, could be an Israelite. As we see in the book of Acts, the Law's circumcision requirement was the most difficult obstacle which had to be overcome before non-Jews could be received into the church. On this question there was no difficulty with the Samaritans. The Jews completely admitted that the Samaritans very meticulously observed the same Law that the Jews recognized.[56] If the gospel of Luke was addressed to the Samaritans, among others, it no doubt emphasized (for this reason) in the first place the necessity of the outpouring of the Holy Spirit upon the Samaritan converts, even including Simon Magus who had earlier called magical powers his own. This was because Luke considered the legalism of the Samaritan priests to be even more lifeless than that of the Pharisees. The Law even reached to John the Baptist, the son of a Zadokite priest of Jerusalem. Would Luke have considered it really necessary to emphasize the end of legalism and to emphasize the necessity of the Spirit, if he wrote for gentiles who did not know the Law before they were confronted with the gospel? Is it not more likely that he wrote for the Samaritans? One must not forget that the Samaritan priestly group did not represent all of Samaritanism. I have the impression that the gospel of John [p.76] was also interested in showing the significance of the gospel for the fulfillment of Samaritan hopes, but that it, as far as it had the Samaritans in mind, addressed itself to the then heretical and more speculative group of the Dositheans.[57]

Both the gospels of Luke and John therefore attempt to give a solution to the Samaritan problem which the early church confronted in two different ways. In my opinion, the distinctive styles of the kerygma in Luke and John are completely explained without restraint from here on out. They were conditioned by the special kind of Samaritanism to which both evangelists addressed themselves.

A Samaritan Decalogue Inscription on the wall of the Hizn Yakub Mosque. Note the possible Christian graffito in the center of the ayin (on the third row from the bottom). Dr. Bowman speculates that this was perhaps done by a Christian Crusader in imitation of his shield, i.e. ⛉ .

The same inscription with Dr. Bowman pushing aside the foilage which covered it. Note that the stone has been placed in the wall upside down.

CHAPTER IV

"The Samaritans and the Sect of Qumran" [p.77]

I have earlier said that Samaritanism from the last centuries B.C. and until about the 14th century A.D. was divided into two main groups.[1] In any case, there was at the same time that the Qumran sect existed the group of the Sabu'ai, which was a rigid old style priestly group, and the Dositheans, a group of priestly origin, who, besides possessing their own views about the correct halakah of the priests, also made use of mystic books and secret statements of faith which were accessible only to the initiated.

It is possible that the original Dosithean sect must not only be considered to have been influenced by Qumran, but also it is even possible that it was founded by the same circles from which the sects of Damascus and Qumran originated. If one thinks about it, one cannot fail to notice that the origin of Samaritanism, as a religious community separated from Judaism, was the result of a rigorous purification of the priesthood of Jerusalem by Ezra. Two hundred years later a few of the Zadokites of Jerusalem may have travelled to Shechem in order to reunite with the members of their family, who after their forced separation from the post-exilic community at the time of Ezra had brought Law there.[2] These Zadokites, who had remained behind in Jerusalem until the Hellenistic period and had kept up with the times, would be happy to discover that the Zadokites who had lived in Shechem since the time of Ezra had preserved the old customs, and in this way they could prove that they were never the heretics Ezra had considered them to be.

It is certainly very difficult to completely reconstruct the dogmas and the customs of the Samaritan Dositheans. As we have already shown earlier,[3] about the 14th century the Dosithean teaching and the old Sabu'ai or original Samaritan customs were bound together into a new unity. So one can find more parallels to Qumran in a modern Samaritan manual like the Malef, than in the sparse notes about the Dositheans in Abu'l Faṭh, Epiphanius, Masudi, and Shahrastani.[4] For these [p.78] authors were either outsiders, who knew nothing about the true teachings of the sect, or they were like Abu'l Faṭh,[5] who diminished the significance of the sect in order to be able to show that orthodox Samaritanism had always been as it was at his time. If there was, therefore, in the time in which the Qumran sect existed two major opposing groups in Samaritanism, and if Qumran had any influence on Samaritanism; then it can be assumed that this influence could not have extended as far or in the same way to both groups. On the contrary, it could be that the Dosithean sect, whose founders appeared at the time of the emigration of the Qumran-Zadokites or in the time after that, was more open to influences from the Qumran sect than the Sabu'ai.

As far as the priesthood was concerned, the Samaritans agreed with the sects of Damascus and Qumran that Zadokite priests were necessary for a legitimate priesthood. The sects of Damascus and Qumran, and also apparently the Samaritan Dositheans, restricted the power of the priesthood with regard to the control of their respective communities. The sectarians of Damascus even granted the name "Zadokites" to their nonpriestly members. In the sect of Qumran we find three priests as compared with twelve laymen (1 QS VIII, 1), and in the council of the sect of Damascus we find four priests as compared to six laymen (Dam. X, 4ff.). This is similar to the Samaritan Dosithean sect. At the time of Baba the number of priestly representatives in the council amounted to three as opposed to four laymen. At least in the sect of Qumran only the sons of Aaron had authority in questions of the law and of property, although the laymen were strongly superior in number to them in the council. In the Samaritan Dosithean sect, as has been said, the number of the priests and laymen were approximately equal. Nevertheless, the voice of the laity appears to have had more importance here, if we may go according to what Abu'l Fatḥ tells us about the work of the council of Baba, quite apart from the role which is assigned to the layman Joshua as opposed to the high priests in the Dosithean inspired Samaritan Book of Joshua.[6]

[p.79] The Sabu'ai, the old-Samaritan priestly party, were not influenced by Baba's reforms; and even when Dositheanism was absorbed into orthodox Samaritanism, it was connected by the Dositheans with the loss of lay representation. The priestly theocracy therefore prevailed with complete success.

In the treatment of questions of purity, the sect of Qumran and both Samaritan sects stand very close to one another. We should remember that the Dosithean sects were much stricter on the whole in questions of purity than the common Samaritans;[7] although occasionally an opposite tendency is perceived, in the sense of a counter-reaction. Above all, before detailed laws about purity are mentioned, it must be pointed out that both the Samaritans and the people of Qumran were convinced that they were children of the light and that only they were pure, but that all others were impure. This belief, which no doubt united the Samaritans of both sects, as well as the Zadokites,[8] was based upon the conviction, on the one hand, that they alone possessed the real Torah and, on the other hand, that only they had an intact priesthood, and that through them they were also provided with the only correct interpretation of the Torah. In the same way, they were certain to be heirs of the covenant through their priests, above all of that covenant of eternal priesthood which had been given to Phinehas. In questions of the halaḵah all were equally severe. Thus both the sects of Damascus and the Samaritans condemned marriage with one's niece while it was permitted by rabbinic Judaism.[9]

The Samaritanism of the 14th century knew, as we have already seen,[10] the teaching of the "sons of light" which is also found in the Manual of Discipline of Qumran. It reached far beyond the conception that each individual sect possessed the correct priesthood and the correct interpretation of the Law. All the Samaritans considered themselves to be potential sons of the light, and likewise all the Qumran-people did too--it made no difference whether they were priests or laymen. But the Samaritan teaching of the sons of light is not a teaching of the old Samaritan priestly sect. The priesthood was traced back to Adam in the Tolidah, whose "chain of the priests" was compiled at the earliest in the first part of the 12th century.[11] Here the pure line of descent of the priesthood is explained and much care is employed on the complete enumeration of the Jubilee years between Adam and Abraham and Moses. The conception that the whole Samaritan community [p.80] consisted of sons of light, however, goes even further beyond the Tolidah or the genealogical tree of the priests. As surely as the official valid line of priests is considered to be the pure line, so there is no doubt that if this principle is expanded to the community, a decline of the authority of the priests or a blurring of the difference between priests and laymen would result, and indeed that is discernible in Dositheanism and the sect of Qumran.

The teaching of the Dosithean sect about the generations of the light can be inferred from the Samaritan hymns of the 14th century[12] and the late Malef Manual. Both contain Dositheam teachings which are accepted today in Samaritan circles. In this connection, the section 1 QS III, 13-IV, 26--which deals with the different groups of men and the two spirits under whose leadership they walk--has not been paid enough attention until today. Erroneously Brownlee inserts the word "consecutive" into 1 QS III, 13 before "generations of all mankind".[13] It is said there that the wise one should teach all the sons of light in all the generations of man, i.e. their different generations not only in vertical lines but also in different groups, as they live together at a given time through the generations. In line 13 "betoledot" is used, but in line 14 "bedorotam" is used. The last word Brownlee translates with "societies", and the first with "generations". It would be more correct if he had done it exactly vice versa [i.e. "bedorotam" = generations and "betoledot" = societies]. The meaning which Brownlee finds in this section, however, is fundamentally the same that I also obtained from it. So far, however, nothing has been said about the two spirits of light and darkness. I now assume that in line 14 the words, "in reference to the various kinds of spirits with their special characteristics", refer to the different groups of men and spirits which are here considered to be intermediate beings existing outside of mankind.

Therefore could the immediately following reference to "their trials and the time of their prosperity" have something to do with the Times of Divine Disfavour and Divine Favour? It appears, however, [p.81] that the "trials" were meant to be eschatological and that the "time of prosperity" was not expected until after the last trial.

The author of the Manual of Discipline then stresses that everything which exists and will be, comes from God. God has determined the purpose of all things before they were created. So they would fulfill what was apportioned to them in agreement with God's predetermined plan. One could change nothing, everything is subject to His lordship, and He preserves everything. After that it is described how God created Man to rule over the world and how He assigned two spirits to him until the time of his affliction, i.e. his trial. These spirits, the spirit of truth and the spirit of corruption, existed outside of man. The author turns again to the _Toledot_-generations or to the consecutive groups of men.[14] There were two groups of men--the generations of truth (_toledot ha-'emet_) and the generations of corruption (_toledot ha'avel_). The first had their origin in the source of the light, the latter in the source of the darkness. The prince of light rules over all the sons of truth, but the angel of darkness rules over all the sons of corruption. The sons of truth walked in the light and the sons of corruption walked in darkness. It is further said that the angel of darkness and the spirits which serve him constantly attack the sons of light. God and his angel of truth would have helped all the sons of light, but now the angel of darkness has the power. Indeed God has created both spirits--that of light and that of darkness, and each work is based on them; however he loves the one spirit and his kind but hates the counsel of the other spirit. Nevertheless it is not especially emphasized that he hates the spirit of darkness itself. It is significant that in III, 25f. both kinds of spirits existed before man. While man is no doubt ruled by them and no man is immune from the attacks of the angel of darkness, a genetic connection appears to be assumed between the sons of light and the sons of darkness and their respective leaders. The result of all this is that some men are destined to be saved and others are destined to damnation. A fierce struggle is fought for the souls of the sons of light by the sons of darkness, and the result of the struggle is not yet known; however, it has always been known what would become of the sons of darkness.

Column IV of the Manual of Discipline reports the details about the nature of the Spirit of truth according to whose counsel the sons of truth walk in the world, and who will give them "peace and descendants in this world, eternal exultations in the [p.82] victorious life of eternity, and a crown of glory with a robe of grandeur in eternal light" (IV, 7f.).

After that the works of the Spirit of corruption are enumerated. The result of its conduct is misfortune and affliction in the fire of the region of darkness. Their descendants (here Brownlee can by no means translate <u>dorot</u>--"generations"--with "societies") would suffer misfortune and catastrophes and will finally be completely destroyed.

IV, 15-26 refers back to the division of mankind into two groups--that of the sons of light and the sons of darkness. Now it is said that God has created hostility between these two groups as well as between their angelic leaders. However he has established a limit. Injustice and the evil-doers would be destroyed at a time established by God, and Truth would win the day. Therefore evil may rule but only until the previously appointed time of judgment--then God will purge a part of mankind while he "will sprinkle him with a spirit of truth like purifying water, in order to cleanse him of the spirit of impurity" (IV, 21). Naturally here the cultic practice of sprinkling someone with water in case of impurity is spiritualized. But this act is reserved for the time of the end, and the passage does not precisely say that real "water of impurity" was in use by the members of the covenant. The following picture of the future is then sketched out: After men are washed clean, they will have a better understanding of God's omniscience and wisdom. They will be elected to an eternal covenant and will receive a share of the glory which Adam possessed before his fall.

It is entirely possible that the members of the covenant believed themselves to be already in the time of the end, and thought that this purification and cleansing was already taking place in them now. It could even be that they considered themselves already purified, and they were convinced that they already possessed all the glory of Adam in his sinless condition. In any case, it is certain that they felt themselves to be in preparation for this condition. For it is admitted that as sons of light they were still attacked by the angel of darkness.

If we turn back to Samaritanism here, we find no parallels to this teaching of the battle of the angels over the souls of men and also nothing about the division of mankind into two camps with each under a single angelic leader (indeed neither in the Samaritan Pentateuch nor the Samaritan Targum nor in the section about the angels in the Kitab al-Tabaḥ of Abu'l Hassan from the 11th century A.D.). We should certainly not expect to find such teachings in any of these writings because they originated from the old Samaritan priestly groups. As we have already seen, [p.83] this group approached a teaching of pure descent in connection with the priestly lineage. On the other hand, parallels to views found in the Manual of Discipline are found in the modern Samaritan Malef collection as well as in the Asatir and the Molad Moshe.[15]

The teachings of the Malef are not new. They are found in liturgical orders of the 14th century and later and to a certain degree in the Memar Marqah of the 4th century A.D. Probably Marqah was influenced by the prevailing Dosithean teaching from Baba's reign.[16] So it is not strange to find Dosithean teachings--after the unification of old Samaritanism and Dositheanism in the 14th century--expressed in the Samaritanism of modern times, in their liturgy, and even in the Malef, which is a catechism of the 19th century.

The Malef begins with the recollection that God said "Let there be light." Here we must recall earlier statements[17] in order to understand what this statement would contain for a Samaritan and what conclusions followed from it for him. The light which is mentioned here was the Holy Spirit and the pre-existent Moses. Adam and Eve were clothed in this light. Then Belial came in the form of a serpent and seduced Eve. As a result Adam lost his clothing of light and obtained the fleshly clothing in which the evil impulse was hidden, which he had received from Eve and which she in turn had received from Belial. Adam and Eve were driven from the Garden, and Cain and Abel were born. Cain and his descendants are the sons of Belial.

After Adam had fulfilled a Nazirite vow for a long time, he begat Seth who was a man in the image of God. Seth's descendants formed the holy chain. The light, which still remained in Adam after the Fall, was handed down through the holy chain to Moses who was the incarnate light. Moses brought the Law and the rule of life which is guarded by the cherubim who were placed at the gates of Eden and over the Ark of the Covenant. By the Law, the Samaritans, who are the sons of light, potentially recovered the status of Adam before the Fall. Of course, they could not obtain the clothing of light until after the resurrection and after the fleshly clothing was judged.

This sketch includes without question a few contacts with Qumran. One especially important one is that it also belonged to the goals of the Qumran movement [p.84] to recover the status of Adam before the Fall.[18] Beyond that, there were further similarities.

Both the Samaritans and the people of Qumran considered themselves to be sons of light, while everyone else was considered to be sons of Belial or darkness. According to the opinion of both parties, there was no hope for other men. That is clearly shown by Marqah in the Midrash to Deut. 32:35: The evil ones and all non-Samaritans will be raised from the dead only to eternal damnation. The same thought is also present in 1 QS IV. With regard to Moses and the Fall of Man, about which the Manual of Discipline is silent, the Samaritans surpass the conceptions of the Qumran people. One of the Dositheans sects--the _Saduqai_[19]--believed that the winged dragon will rule over all creatures up to the day of the resurrection. This can be compared with the fact that according to 1 QS III,

20-23 the evil angel has authority up to the time of judgment. According to the Manual of Discipline, the angel of light watches over the children of light. In the Samaritan sources the Angel of light is, to be sure, not mentioned. However, according to the Malef, the Holy Spirit and Moses are clearly the Light. Also one should take into consideration that the Samaritan liturgy says that Moses prays now and at the end of time for the Samaritans.[20] Therefore perhaps Moses is the Samaritan equivalent of the angel of light. Thus there are, on the one hand, obvious differences between the Samaritan Dosithean conceptions of the sons of light and of darkness and those of Qumran; but, on the other hand, they have many agreements.

The sect of Qumran had teachings which were only destined for their initiates and which must not be revealed to outsiders. Earlier we mentioned[21] that the Saduqai, one of the Samaritan Dosithean sects, required their members to keep silent and to reveal to no outsiders the inner secrets of their "ways".[22] It would certainly not have been difficult for the people of Qumran to have been absorbed by one of the Samaritan Dosithean sects after the destruction of Qumran. It clearly follows from their Manual of Discipline that they not only generally required the fulfillment of the Pentateuchal laws and the observance of Pentateuchal prohibitions, but they also made use of certain esoteric teachings and attached great importance to having them carefully followed by their initiates.[23] The same phenomenon is directly found in a [p.85] striking way among the Samaritans. Besides the traditional creed, the Malef knows a holy history of the sect and an original stock of especially secret teaching which is made known to the

Samaritan children. This conjunction of belief and gnosis is something which first the Samaritan Dositheans and later the Samaritans as a whole have in common with the people of Qumran.

Both the Qumran sect and the Samaritans considered Deut. 18:18 to be a messianic text. The Samaritan Ta'eb and the messiah of Israel, on the one hand, and the Samaritan high priest from the time of the Ta'eb and the Aaronic messiah, on the other hand, are in many respects parallel phenomena. Thus it is true of the Samaritan high priest that he, with the vessels and the altar of incense which belonged to the original tabernacle and which the Ta'eb will find again, will perform complete atonement for the country. Probably both sects were influenced by Ezekiel's thoughts about the _Nasi_ and the atonement which the Zadokite priests would perform for the country. In the Damascus Document the _Nasi_ is also mentioned.[24] On the other hand, in the Manual of Discipline of Qumran as well as with the Samaritans, messianic hope was based directly on Deut. 18:18. Like the Samaritans, the followers of the Qumran sect were opposed to the temple at Jerusalem and hoped for a new sanctuary, and the Samaritan Dosithean sect never approved of the Samaritan temple as long as it stood on Mount Gerizim.[25] Significantly, after their own temple was destroyed, they placed their hopes on the restoration of the original Tabernacle.

Moses was given a special place by Qumran as well as by the Samaritans. Because of the enumeration of the promises of a blessing by the priests and the threats of a curse by the Levites,[26] the annual renewal of the covenant by the people of Qumran reminds one of the recitation which took place three times a year by the Samaritans on the occasion of their pilgrimage to Mount Gerizim.[27] Even here there are differences. But a dominant mutuality exists in the fact that the Samaritans [p.86] considered themselves to be the Mosaic sect par excellence, while the Sectarians of Qumran saw themselves as the restorers of the Pentateuchal covenant, and in addition of the covenant, which Joshua and the people had made after the conquest of the land, just as it had been forseen by Moses. Finally, the special Qumran halaḵah[28] may have been, like the Samaritan halaḵah, small in scope, since here as there the emphasis was placed on the fulfillment of the written Law.

A special difficulty for the assumption of relationships between the Samaritans and the Qumran sect appears to lie in the fact that the sectarians of Qumran lived together as a brotherhood while the Samaritans at the same time formed more of a national rather than a religious group. However, one could consider the house of teaching in Shechem/Nablus which was built by Baba in the neighborhood of the synagogue and the *Mikweh* as a kind of maternal home of Samaritan Dositheanism. There Baba, his priests, and learned laymen (who were members of his council) studied the Torah and pronounced judgements; and the members of the council went out from there in order to supervise the different districts allotted to them. There those who wanted to become members in the council were also examined for their fitness. Certainly we must not stress such parallels too much. If the school house in Shechem/Nablus was truly a kind of maternal home of Samaritan Dositheanism,[29] then it was, in comparison with the rest of the Samaritan community (which was a national community), much smaller than the Qumran settlement, in comparison with the urban or rural groups outside of this center. In addition, we can only postulate, on the basis of an analogy with the Essenes, the existence of scattered groups such as those which were connected with Qumran. In reality Qumran--unlike Baba's center in Shechem/Nablus--was at the same time the central point and entire territory of the sectarians at the Dead Sea.

We know that the Samaritans had Nazirites since there were Samaritan Nazirites even in the Middle Ages.[30] As was noted earlier,[31] it was important for the Samaritans that the Nazirite term lasted 366 plus 7 more days [i.e. 373 days]. In their eyes, a Nazirite had the same degree of purity as the high priest. [p.87] One may assume that the Dosithean Samaritans had an interest in the general dissemination of Naziritism. Thus the earlier mentioned story of Dusis and Yahdu[32] seems to show that Dusis had taken up an existing inclination to aceticism and had made it the basis for a kind of Naziritism. Perhaps the only reason the Dosithean heresy found an opening into Samaritanism at all was because it further developed and completed the previously existing Pentateuchal system concerning Naziritism. Certainly it is very interesting that Yusuf b. Salama mentions male and female Nazirites and reports that they lived together in a community. He even knows of a cohabitation of Nazirites, consecrated by God, with priests. Here we have in the Nazirite system, as it was developed by the Samaritans, therefore a kind of regular monastic life. The female Nazirites did not necessarily live in the same houses as the male Nazirites. In any case, no sexual relationships were permitted during the time of one's Naziritism, as Yusuf b. Salama emphasizes in reference to Noah's life on the ark. The Nazirite vows could be renewed from time to time by the Samaritans, however one could also be a Nazirite for life.[33]

The normal length of time for Samaritan Naziritism was derived by Gematria from col yeme nizro (כל ימי נזרו) and was therefore fixed at 373 days. That is mentioned by Yusuf b. Salama in his 11th century handbook.[34] There he mentions the guiding principles and rites of the priests. He also quotes the opinions of others, whom he does not name as a rule, only in order to refute them. So in the section on questions of purity, he criticizes the views of those who believe that one will become unclean if the shadow of a grave falls on one. This is a view of the Dustan sect, as we have noted from Abu'l Faṭh.[35] Concerning the duration of being a Nazirite, he gives different reasons why it should include 373 days; among them that this time span results from a full year of 366 plus 7 days, in which the 7 additional days of time would correspond to the consecration of the high priest whom the Nazirite equalled in purity. [p.88] Is this a Dosithean view?[36] In his "machine-like" translation of Yusuf b. Salama's Kafi, the deceased Moses Gaster said about Chap. 19, in which Naziritism is dealt with, that the fact that both the Jubilee year and the term of being a Nazirite, according to the Samaritan interpretation, comprised one year and 7 days shows that both are based upon a year with months of 31 days. Gaster goes even further and points out that the Samaritan Nazirites and the sect which introduced the Jubilee year had many things in common. According to Yusuf b. Salama, they derived this unit of time from Noah who was confined for a year. However, traditions appear to have been known by the Samaritan sects which were also used in the Book of Jubilees. Thus the Tolidah, the genealogy of the old Samaritan group of priests, gives the same age for some of the Patriarchs from the time before the flood as that given by the Book of Jubilees.[37]

It may be that Naziritism, both in the Qumran sect as well as in the Samaritan Dositheans, was customary as a kind of training before admission to full membership in each sect. No precise statements can be made concerning the equivalent custom of Naziritism among the Dositheans, since none of the rules for initiation into this sect are known. But we do know that in Qumran a novitiate had to serve two years of preparation before he could become a full member. Thus in the first year the "Purity of the Many" was denied to him.[38] Does that mean that he had to take the Nazirite vow for a year before he obtained admission to the _me_ _nidda_, because only those whose purity was guaranteed were allowed to use it? At any rate, only at the end of the required time of Naziritism would he be sprinkled with the _me_ _nidda_.[39] Subsequently it must be considered possible that the first year of preparation in Qumran was modelled on Naziritism. But if that was the case, then the fact is significant that in Samaritanism one year was the fundamental span of time for Naziritism. It will be noted in the remaining section that we can find nothing in the Bible which says that the period of Naziritism should last one year. It is no less important that not all the Samaritans agreed concerning the length of that year. Therefore a special teaching is clearly present here.

The second year of preparation in Qumran can be absolutely defined by a second Nazirite vow. At the end of the first year one obtained a share in the "Purity of the Many", but at the end of the second, he also obtained a share in the wine of the "Many", and not until then would one first be authorized to eat and drink with the community. [p.89] As everyone knows, abstention from wine was part of what characterized the Nazirite.

On the other hand, among the Samaritans the Nazirite not only abstains, but he is supposed to concentrate positively on spiritual things and keep his thoughts pure. Perhaps one can recognize a parallel to a similar phenomenon in the Naziritism of Qumran, in this additional positive content of Samaritan Naziritism, if it was a duty of the novitiates to study the Torah and to be introduced to the teachings of the sect there. It is possible that here is an example that Nazirite laws could very easily lead to the cloistered life of an entire Nazirite group under the supervision of the priests. But this must not have been an original development in the sect of Qumran, any more than such a custom needed to be introduced into Samaritanism from the outside by Dusis. Dusis could have promoted such a development; however, it remains a fact that even Yusuf b. Salama, who was a priest and member of the orthodox priestly party, had knowledge of the cohabitation of orthodox Samaritan priests with Nazirites. Perhaps the Dositheans in theory modified the teaching about the Nazirites but in practice kept the Nazirite obligations. Therefore it could be that the existence of the Nazirites in a one year Nazirite fellowship directed by the priests goes back to a Zadokite heritage which was common to the Samaritans and Qumran. Yusuf b. Salama says that only the Samaritan high priest could release a Samaritan Nazirite from his vow.[40] Can one conclude then that the Dositheans, who did not acknowledge the high priest, had great difficulties if they wanted to give up their Naziritism?

I would like to return now to the _me nidda_ mentioned above, i.e. the water of purification which was obtained from the ashes of the red heifer. Since the Samaritans had maintained the rite of burning of the red heifer and furthermore were able to produce the ashes of purification, they could prepare the *me nidda* which was necessary for the performance of the ritual of purification. Even the sacrifice could be offered by their priests irrespective of whether their temple still stood or not. After the destruction of their temple, the Samaritans passed through a very difficult time until they found their way again. But the offerings, including the Passover offering, could be made just as before. In 1958 I published an article which demonstrated the possibility that the red heifer was also burned in Qumran.[41] In addition, there are in Qirbet Qumran a significant number of baptismal installations (*Mikwa'ot*). Now Josephus mentions frequent bathings [p.90] as characteristic of the Essenes,[42] but he gives no details about their rites of purification. At any rate, for a priestly sect like the Zadokites of Qumran, the immersions in the ritual bath (*Mikweh*) would certainly not have been sufficient if one wanted to satisfy the biblical laws of purification. For certain basic purifications the *me nidda* were indispensable.

The Mishnah knows about the high degree of purity which was required if someone wanted to apply the water of purification.[43] An entire tractate was devoted to the preparation of the ashes (*Parah*), but it hardly says anything about the cases in which the *me nidda* were used. At the time that the Mishnah was written, one could certainly no longer obtain the *me nidda*, since the priesthood of the temple of Jerusalem no longer held office, and the red heifer could only be burned on the Mount of Olives by Jerusalem priests of a certain degree of purification. The tradition has preserved reminiscences that the Rabbis, when the temple still stood, interfered with the proceedings of the priests and arranged for the red heifer to be burned according to Pharisaic rules. This shows that already at the time of the second temple they sought to gain a decisive influence on priestly actions. There is no ultimate basis for that in the self-consciousness of Pharisaism or the Rabbis who were influenced by it. Although the Rabbis were to some extent like the laity even when dealing with quite everyday matters, they assigned to themselves purity requirements which were just as high as the priests when they dealt with holy things. Thereby the Rabbis could naturally not get along without the priests; so they and others could also not do without the cooperation of the priests in the burning of the red heifer. They were able to organize a wealth of rules concerning purity. But they had to come to terms with the fact that only priests could fulfill the law concerning the red heifer, and then they also had to accept the fact that the _me nidda_ were no longer available when in the year 70 A.D. they took over the spiritual leadership of Judaism. So since that time the Jews have been unclean, in the strict sense of the term, even if they observe all the other rules concerning purification. Maimonides predicted in his commentary on the _Seder Tohorot_ that the first deed of the messiah would be to burn the red heifer, in order to make the ashes available again for the water of purification and to cleanse Israel with it. Since the Samaritans burned the red heifer up until the Middle Ages, Yusuf b. Salama could accuse the Jews and Judaism of not only being unclean but also of separating themselves from Israel since they did not burn the red heifer.

In the above named article [_Revue de Qumran_ 1 (1958), pp. 73-84], I have attempted to show that the Qumran sect supported the thesis in their Manual of Discipline that the Rabbis could not be clean without [p.91] the ashes of the red heifer. It appears to me that the Manual of Discipline refers here to certain component parts of the oral interpretation of the Torah as it was later collected and edited in the Mishnah tractate _Mikwa'ot_. According to it, the sea could serve as a baptistry. On the other hand, the Manual of Discipline insists that even sea water could not be purified.[44] I do not consider it impossible that the sect also advocated a spiritualizing of baptism [sprinkling with water] for it appeals to Ezek. 36: 25ff.--incorrectly, to be sure, because Ezekiel neither spiritualizes the priestly act of atonement nor even treats it metaphorically in the Zadokite manifesto. Therefore it should not be considered impossible that the sect of Qumran really produced and used the _me nidda_. One did not need an altar in order to burn the red heifer, for this could only take place, according to the Pentateuchal laws, "outside of the camp".[45]

The sect of Qumran, as well as the Samaritans, consequently had their own special haggadah to which one must bind himself, while the rabbinic haggadah was not binding. A metaphoric or haggadic interpretation of the baptism [sprinkling with water] could be very close to the real execution of the ritual. On the other hand, the rabbinate did not interpret the Pentateuchal commandments about immersion metaphorically, even on the lowest level of the doctrine of purification, as the tractate _Mikwa'ot_ proves. An early Jerusalem Zadokite halakah may very well be preserved in the Samaritan halakah concerning the water of purification. It shows an unbroken priestly custom and the central position of the _me nidda_ in a community which is ruled by priests. The Samaritan system, with its emphasis on purity, still reflects the original significance of the red heifer and makes it possible to understand references in the Manual of Discipline referring to the me nidda which could not be adequately explained from the rabbinic-mishnaic halakah, since these originated from a time in which the performance of the entire rites of purification was no longer possible.

Therefore a fundamental relationship existed between the Samaritan community and the community of Qumran in that in both communities the priests really had some say.[46] Dosithean Samaritanism, the Sect of Damascus, and even the Sect of Qumran have from here on out more in common [p.92] with one another than with the old Samaritan priestly group, the Sabuʿai, because the priests did not belong to Dositheanism, and the sects at the Dead Sea stood under absolute priestly control.

For a priest, Levitical purity is fundamental. It is first of all a goal in itself, but in addition it is also important for certain religious acts because they would be invalid if they were not performed in a condition of complete ritual purity. But there is still another essential factor for valid religious acts, namely that they be performed at the correct time. That is why such great importance is ascribed to the correct calendar in the Hebrew sphere. As the calendar of the people, the calendar is the calendar of God: "The festivals of the Lord, which you shall proclaim, these are my festivals."[47] Among the Samaritans the priests have maintained their control over the calendar, and even today twice a year they publish the calendar for the next six months. As has already been said,[48] that takes place on the Sabbath of Zimmut Pesah and the Sabbath of Zimmut Sukkot; therefore eight

Sabbaths before the Passover in Shebaṭ and eight Sabbaths before Sukkoṯ in Ab. The Samaritans were confronted, like the Jews, with the problem of reconciling the lunar year and the solar year with one another, since they both had to follow the Pentateuchal instructions concerning the times of the festivals. On the one hand, the festivals were based upon the full moon, as is the case, for example, with the Passover-full moon in Nisan and the Sukkoṯ-full moon in Tishri; and, on the other hand, they are also based on the times of the year with their fruits. So the first gift of barley is to be offered either on the day after the Sabbath which follows the Passover (as the Samaritans do), or on the day after the Passover (as rabbinic Jews do). Sukkoṯ, on the other hand, is for both Samaritans and Jews the appointed time for the presentation of the autumn fruits. Probably the Jerusalem priests learned to perform calendrical calculations in the post-exilic period, especially since the Babylonian priests had much earlier learned to perform astronomical calculations.[49] The Jewish priests who stayed in Babylon probably could not fail to notice that the conjunctions of the sun and moon which took place twice a year were separated by six months. From Ezekiel's Zadokite manifesto, it is clear that the Passover and the Feast of Tabernacles are both major festivals which to a certain extent coincide with the spring and autumn equinoxes. Could Ezekiel's references to Jerusalem as the navel of the world[50] have a priestly-astronomical [p.93] basis? The Samaritans stressed that they alone had the correct calendar, because their observations were conducted from the correct place. When the Zadokites left Jerusalem about 180 B.C., they no doubt took the priestly calendrical secrets with them. Then the Pharisees at that time probably did not receive possession of the calendrical secrets. It is also doubtful whether the Maccabean priesthood and the Sadducees knew the calendrical secrets of the Zadokite priests.

If we can trust the statements of the Mishnah, the intervention of the Rabbis in calendrical affairs was only possible because the Sadducees did not know the old priestly calendrical calculations. In any case, the Rabbis did not receive full control over the calendar until after the year 70 A.D. when Rabbi Johanan ben Zakkai called his Sanhedrin in Jabnia. But even then the controversy was not yet settled as far as the Rabbis were concerned. Probably that first happened under Gamliel II when Joshua ben Hananiah dealt with the calendrical questions on a large scale. The Rabbis determined their calendars up to the 5th century by empirical observation of the moon. The Mishnah tractate Rosh ha-Shanah in any case represents rabbinic usage.[51] They fixed the beginning of a new month by observation of the new moon in Jerusalem. Probably some statements in the Mishnah tractate Rosh ha-Shanah even guarantee that previously, when the temple still existed, the calendar was calculated empirically by the observation of the new moon in Jerusalem.[52] I suppose that at the time of the conjunctions of the sun and moon in Shebaṭ and in Ab one remembered the old Zadokite order of the temple. For the Pharisees, therefore, it was of the greatest importance to divert attention from those times. They were the times of the temple sacrifices in which one prepared oneself for the major festivals--Passover and the Feast of Tabernacles--and they were probably also important for the priests, on the basis of the calendar. If one wanted to prove the authority and independence of one's own religious community, the best pre-requisite in the old Jewish sphere was to have one's own calendar. So the 15th Shebaṭ was made by the Rabbis the "New Year of Trees". As a new festival on the eleventh of Adar close to the preceding full moon in Nisan, the festival of Purim was installed, whose festival legend, the Book of Esther, was written at the time of the Maccabean revolt in order to awaken national sentiment. Above all, it was essential to observe at least the full moon of the month which preceded Nisan. There was only a slight remembrance of the 15th of Ab.[53] On this day, one once would have sacrificed a gift of wood for the altar and celebrated a great feast of joy. [p.94] Moreover, it once had been a favorable date for calendrical calculations, which fell on the early autumn conjunction of the sun and moon. However, the secret of such calculations was forgotten. As a result Hannukah, at the winter solstice two months after the end of the Feast of Tabernacles, took the place of the 15th of Ab which was precisely two months before the Feast of Tabernacles.

The Samaritan Zadokite priests honored everything with respect to the old Zadokite systems of the temple of the Shebaṭ and Ab full moons. They collected their Sheḳalim and temple sacrifice and also gave their calendar a historical foundation. So the Sabbath of Ẓimmut Pesaḥ was and will be for the Samaritan the day of remembrance of the meeting between Moses and Aaron after Moses returned from Midian, and it also commemorated the first announcement of the coming deliverance; while the Sabbath of Ẓimmut Sukkoṯ was considered to be the day of remembrance of the meeting of Moses, Aaron and Eleazar, when Aaron died and Eleazar took his place as the priest of Israel. The Samaritan priestly lineage, which is traced back through Zadok to Eleazar and further back to Aaron, no doubt preserves here a Zadokite priestly recollection that the office of priest was given to their ancestors for all time.

But the Samaritan priests' right to make decisions concerning the calendar was not always undisputed. It can be inferred from Abu'l Fatḥ's first report about the Dusis-sect that the Dositheans refused to use astronomical tables to compute the calendar.[54] According to them all months should have 30 days, and Pentecost is supposed to be calculated to lie (as with the Jews) on the 50th day from the morning of Passover. Abu'l Fatḥ further reports that the Dositheans absolutely abolished all the festivals except for the Sabbath. Abolition, or rather an alteration of the festivals,[55] appears to have been a characteristic of the major varieties of the Dusis sect.[56] If the Dusis sects were inspired by Qumran, then their tendency to abolish the festivals would be difficult to understand. The sect of Qumran, on their part, did not abolish the festivals; they only insisted that one celebrate them at the correct time. The Manual of Discipline does not reveal the secret of the Qumran calendar. But probably it was once said that when the sun and moon stood in conjunction and in the same house that this was the door to the time of the festivals.[57] In a certain way, this passage suggests a similarity to the Samaritan conception of the Ẓimmut Pesaḥ, which in the Samaritan liturgy was often called the "Door of the Festivals". One [p.95] might miss the relationship which exists here, if one stresses too much that the Qumran year was a solar and not a lunar year. Like the Samaritan year, the year in Qumran was essentially a solar year, but there was still a close relationship between the solar and lunar year. The Rabbinic Jewish year, on the other hand, was a purely lunar year.

So there were also discussions among the sects as to whether to put more emphasis on the lunar or solar year. Neither inclination could disregard the other completely. The Jews helped themselves further by inserting a second month, Adar, in each third year of their cycle of nineteen years in order to avoid too great a divergence of solar and lunar years. This is still done today.

My opinion is that both the calendar of the Samaritan old priestly group and the calendar of Qumran go back to a Zadokite method of calendrical calculation. Neither of the two groups celebrated Purim or Hanukkah. A difference exists between them only in the calculation of Pentecost, and both appear to be acquainted with the calendar of the Book of Jubilees.[58] The Samaritans even calculate their years, just like the Book of Jubilees, according to the years of Jubilees. In addition, the Book of Jubilees appears to give special importance to Pentecost. It is believed that the calendar of Qumran may have been identical to that of the Book of Jubilees and had a solar calendar with Pentecost as a major festival. But here the similarity is overemphasized. However it may be related to the Book of Jubilees, Pentecost by no means has the central place in the calendar of the Manual of Discipline. The Samaritans and the sect which produced the Book of Jubilees as well as the Manual of Discipline of Qumran reveal only a certain similarity in chronological questions, however they agree from time to time on other crucial points. So the Samaritans and the Manual of Discipline appear to have had a six month festival year which was governed by the conjunctions of the sun and moon.[59] On the other hand, the Manual of Discipline says nothing about the meeting of Moses with Aaron which took place on Ẓimmut.

Finally, it is of interest that the rabbinic Jews determined their year on the basis of the conjunction of the sun and moon, in the course of which they prepared it according to the work of Jarḥinai, one of the Jewish astronomers who lived in the 5th century A.D. in Babylon. Perhaps the old family of Zadokites, from whom the Samaritans [p.96] and the sectarian people of the Dead Sea originated, had learned of this conjunction already a thousand years before in the same place, i.e. Babylon.

The relationships between the Samaritans, in so far as it concerned the old priestly Samaritan sect, and the sectarians of Qumran consisted in a common priestly heritage in purity and calendrical matters. The other wing of Samaritanism--the Dositheean gnostics--emphasized that they were all sons of light and had a guardian angel. They are convinced that the present world is subject to Belial, that a judgment will come, and that the faithful would recover the lost bodies of light. Qumran had all this in common with the Dosithean wing of Samaritanism. Even when something was modified, religious practice still conformed to the old Zadokite priestly heritage, which possessed only a few articles of faith besides belief in God and the veneration of Moses: the Torah, Gerizim, Bethel, and the expectation of a day of reckoning and reward. Faith in this sense was as such the gift of Qumran and similar sects to the Samaritans. The pure and simple Samaritanism is not to be considered the mother of the gnostic heresies. If we want to look for them, then we must remember the response of Qumran to the dissatisfaction of many Samaritans with the sterile Samaritan legalism, which was more sterile than anything that a later Zadokite priest of Jerusalem like Jesus Sirach or the Zadokite ascetics of Damascus and the Dead Sea produced. Only through the invasion of new ideas from Dositheanism, which (for its part) was influenced by the dissatisfied Jerusalem refugees to whom the Qumran people belonged, has Samaritanism remained alive up until today. It repaid its indebtedness to the former in that it now helps us to put a little light on those who, without intending to do so, helped it to remain alive until today.

NOTES

Notes to Chapter I

"The History of the Samaritans"

[1] 2 Chron. 30:1-11; 31:1.

[2] 2 Kings 23:15-20.

[3] Jer. 41:5.

[4] In Neh. 4:1 Arabs, Ammonites, and Ashdodites are referred to. In Ezra 4:1f. the opponents, who wanted to rebuild the Temple together with Zerubbabel and the Jews, refer to the fact that they have sacrificed to Yahweh "since the time of Esarhaddon, the king of Assyria, who brought us here".

[5] In the enemy's attitude a distinction is made between the reconstruction of the Temple and the reconstruction of the wall. Sanballat was completely ineffectual or even very weak in his opposition (cf. Neh. 3:33; 4:1; 6:1f., 5f.). Perhaps he was compelled to do so because of some reports about messianic attempts, which he feared would come to the attention of the Persian king (cf. Neh. 6:6).

[6] In the year 128 B.C. (cf. Josephus _Ant_. 13:254-256).

[7] Three districts (Aphairema, Lydda, Rathamin) were already united to Judea in 145 B.C. under Jonathan, on the basis of a promise made by Demetrius II, and kept by Antiochus VI (cf. 1 Macc. 10:30, 38; 11:28, 34, 57).

[8] Cf. Josephus, _Ant_. 20, 118ff.; _Bell_. 2, 233.

Notes to pp. 5-10

[9]After the dethronement of Archelaus (6 A.D.), Judea and Samaria were united into a single province, which was put under the Proconsulate of Syria. Pontius Pilate ruled Judea as well as Samaria, but there was a Samaritan council (Josephus, Ant. 18:88f.), probably similar to the Jewish Sanhedrin, which could appeal directly to Rome. This took place, for example, when Pilate's removal was desired.

[10]Cf. Montgomery, Samaritans, p. 89.

[11]Cf. ibid., pp. 90-92.

[12]Cf. ibid., p. 118f.

[13]Cf. ibid., chap. 7: "The Samaritans under Islam", p. 125ff.

[14]Cf. above, p. 14; chap. II, p. 39f.

[15]Cf. Bowman, Ezekiel, p. 9.

[16]Cf. Montgomery, loc. cit., pp. 148-153.

[17]R. Gerschom ben Jehuda in Mainz, named "Me'or ha-Gola", a rabbinic authority of the 10th/11th centuries.

[18]See above, chap. II, p. 32ff.

[19]Joh. 4:22.

[20]Cf. "The Alexander Legend": Lev. R. XIII, 5 to 11:1; Jos. Ant. 11, 321-345; Alexander and the Kingdom of Darkness: T. B. Tam. 31b/32a; the Ascent to Heaven: T. J. AbZ. III, 42c, 53ff.; Num. R. XIII, 14 to 7:13.

[21]A Classical Philologist (1540-1609). His correspondence with the Samaritans stands at the beginning of the scholarly investigation of the history and faith of the Samaritans.

[22]On the year of the rediscovery of the Samaritan Pentateuch by Petro Della Valle, see Gaster, Samaritans, pp. 101, 181-184.

[23]An Evangelical Theologian (1786-1842).

[24]Father and son, an evangelical theologian and learned Hebraist: John the Elder 1564-1629; John the Younger 1599-1664.

[25]A Roman Catholic Theologian (1591-1659).

[26]Cf. Gaster, Samaritans, p. 183.

[27]"Chronique Samaritaine," Journal Asiatique 14 (1869), pp. 385-470. The MS. of the Tolidah which Neubauer used from the Bodleian Library originated from the 19th century.

[28]Bowman, Tolidah.

[29]R. H. Charles, The Book of Jubilees or The Little Genesis, translated from the Editor's Ethiopic Text, 1902, p. LXXVIf.

[30]I Chron. 5:27-41. It is even more amazing that these similarities do not end with Uzzi (5:31), the last priest which the Samaritans concede they have in common with the Jews. They do not conclude even with Zadok and even in the time of the Schism up to the Exile we still find points of contact.

[31]Cf. Josephus, Ant. 11:302f., 306ff.

[32]Neubauer, Chronique, p. 401 (Bowman, Tolidah, p. 14). The second exile came from the East by the king of the Greeks (cf. ibid.). This king is not the Alexander of whom shortly afterwards it is said: "Alexander, the king of Macedonia, came and conquered the whole country."

[33]Neubauer, p. 405 (Bowman, p. 18).

[34]Neubauer, p. 403 (Bowman, p. 15).

[35]Neubauer, p. 403f. (Bowman, p. 16f.).

[36]Num. 25:11-13.

[37]Th. W. J. Juynboll, Chronicon Samaritanum, arabice conscriptum, cui titulus est Liber Josuae.

Notes to pp. 16-18

[38]Cf. M. Gaster, "Das Buch Josua in hebräisch-samaritanischer Rezension," Zeitschrift der Deutschen Morgenländischen Gesellschaft 62 (1908), chap. XXIII and XXIV.

[39]Cf. Th. W. J. Juynboll, loc. cit., chap. 40.

[40]Ibid., chap. 43.

[41]Ibid., chap. 41.

[42]Ibid., chap. 2.

[43]Ibid., chap. 4.

[44]Ibid., chap. 49.

[45]Ibid., chap. 50.

[46]Cf. J. Bowman, "The Exegesis of the Pentateuch among the Samaritans and among the Rabbis," Oudtestamentische Studiën 8 (1950), pp. 220-267.

[47]Cf. in addition Gaster, Samaritans, p. 142f.

[48]Cf. in addition, ibid., pp. 140-142.

[49]Cf. M. Gaster, "Das Buch Josua in hebräisch-samaritanischer Rezension," Zeitschrift der Deutschen Morgenländischen Gesellschaft 62 (1908), chap. XVI-XXI; Th. W. J. Juynboll, loc. cit., chap. XXIII, XXVI and XXXVII. On the Jewish legend cf. M. Soṭ. VIII, 1; T. B. Soṭ. 42b in regard to 2 Sam. 10:16, 18. The Samaritan version, however, appears as a Jewish Midrash in the Sefer juchassin, edited by Filipowski (1857), II, p. 60f.

[50]Cf. Abu'l Fatḥ, Annales Samaritani, edited by E. Vilmar (1865), p. 5 (related to a somewhat contemptuous insinuation cf. ibid., p. 137).

[51]See above, note 38.

[52]Cf. above, pp. 14-15.

[53]Neubauer, Chronique, p. 403ff. (Bowman, Tolidah, p. 17f.).

[54]Although the Tolidah states that in such cases a priest accompanies the laymen, we will come back to the full significance of this statement (see below, pp. 24ff.).

[55]Cf. Th. W. J. Juynboll, *loc. cit.*, chap. 6.

[56]Cf. *ibid.*, chap. 9.

[57]Angels are frequently mentioned in the Samaritan-Arabic Joshua, cf. e.g. *ibid.*, chaps. 3, 10, 17, 19, 29, 41, and 42.

[58]*Ibid.*, chap. 23. On Joshua and the Torah, cf. also chaps. 9 and 10.

[59]*Ibid.*, chap. 26.

[60]*Ibid.*, chap. 24.

[61]*Ibid.*, chap. 41.

[62]*Ibid.*, chaps. 43-44.

[63]*Ibid.*, chap. 45.

[64]*Ibid.*, chap. 45.

[65]*Ibid.*, chap. 46.

[66]*Ibid.*, chap. 47.

[67]*Ibid.*, chap. 48.

[68]*Ibid.*, chap. 50.

[69]Vilmar, p. 139.

[70]*Ibid.*, pp. 125-148.

[71]Th. W. J. Juynboll, *loc. cit.*, chap. 48.

[72]Vilmar, p. 129f.

[73]See above, pp. 14-15.

Notes to pp. 24-29

[74]Vilmar, p. 129f.

[75]*Ibid.*, p. 131.

[76]*Ibid.*, p. 145. Cf. A. E. Cowley, *The Samaritan Liturgy* (1909), Vol. II, p: 43, on the basis of Vilmar, *Abu'l Fath*, p. 179.

[77]Another form of the name Dustis.

[78]Vilmar, p. 151.

[79]*Adv. haer.* XI: "The Sebuaeans choose the new moon of unleavened bread according to the new year, which falls in the autumn...afterwards they choose the beginning of the year, and directly thereafter they celebrate the festival of unleavened bread."

[80]Cf. Montgomery, *Samaritans*, p. 258f.

[81]Cf. Vilmar, *Abu'l Fath*, p. 82.

[82]Cf. Montgomery, *Samaritans*, pp. 253-265.

[83]Wajjescheb §2. Cf. *Pirke de -R. Eliezer*, edited by G. Friedländer (1916), p. 299: R. Dosethai and R. Michaia.

[84]*Ant.* 13, 74-79.

[85]Cf. Montgomery, *Samaritans*, p. 258.

Notes to Chapter II

"The Religion of the Samaritans"

[1]John 4:21.

[2]John 4:22.

[3]Deut. 27:4f. The Samaritan version has "Gerizim" instead of "Ebal" in the M. T. Concerning Gerizim as the mountain of mercy, cf. Deut. 11:29; 27:12.

[4]Cf. J. Bowman, "The Samaritans and the Book of Deuteronomy" in _Transactions of the Glasgow University Oriental Society_ 17 (1957-58), pp. 9-18.

[5]Cf. Bowman, _Ezekiel_.

[6]According to the _Kafi_ of Yusuf b. Salama (11th century A.D.) in the chapter about prayer.

[7]E.g. the altars of Adam, Seth, Isaac, and Noah.

[8]Ex. 23:17. The Samaritan version has "Aron", i.e. the Ark of the Covenant. The visit of the high priest, who is there at the Ark of the Covenant. and the reception of his blessings is the high point of the pilgrimage (cf. Ms. 1111 of the Gaster collection of Samaritan Manuscripts in the John Rylands Library in Manchester).

[9]See below, pp. 41f.

[10]For the text, cf. A. E. Cowley, _The Samaritan Liturgy I_, (Oxford University Press, 1909), beginning.

[11]On the Samaritan tenth commandment, cf. Gaster, _Samaritans_, pp. 185-190.

[12]Therefore in fully developed Rabbinic Judaism there were never formal persecutions of heretics in the manner of the Inquisition (cf. the article "Heresy and Heretics" in _The Jewish Encyclopedia_, VI, p. 353f.). Judaism was and is sensitive where the unity and uniqueness of God is denied. If the separation is inevitable here, then it can or must come also on the basis of serious differences in halaḵic questions (cf. the excommunication of R. Eliezer ben Hyrcanus, because he said an _aknai_-oven could not be unclean; T. B. B. Meẓ. 59 a/b; T. I. M. ḳaṭ 81c, 73ff.).

Notes to pp. 32-35

[13]Cf. now J. Macdonald, Memar Marqah. The Teaching of Marqah (Beihefte zur Zeitschrift für die alttestamentliche Wissenschaft 84) 2 vols. (1963); a brief summary vol. 1, p. XXXIXf.

[14]Cf. Bowman, Ezekiel.

[15]Neubauer, Chronique, p. 392 (Bowman, Tolidah, p. 11).

[16]"Samaritans, Tobiads, and Judahites in Pseudo-Philo," Proceedings of the American Academy for Jewish Research 20 (1951), p. 312. [This work has also been reprinted as a monograph with the title: Samaritans, Tobiads, and Judahites in Pseudo-Philo; Use and Abuse of the Bible by Polemicists and Doctrinaires. New York: The American Academy for Jewish Research, 1951.]

[17]While Hyrcanus is not mentioned in the Samaritan Joshua Book, it is stressed towards the end of chap. 45 (cf. Th. W. J. Juynboll, loc. cit.) that the Samaritans, after their repatriation from the Exile in Persia by Boktonassar, the Persian, refused to comply with the Jewish invitations to participate in the rebuilding of the temple in Jerusalem. They preferred to rebuild their own temple on Mount Gerizim. After Zerubbabel and Sanballat had argued about whether or not Gerizim was the chosen place, and which edition of the Torah was authentic, and after both disputes were decided in favor of the Samaritans, God remembered his covenant and everything was like before the "Time of Divine Disfavour":

> And they built the Holy of Holies like it was in the (old) temple, and they gave a great offering and the earth yielded its fruits and was again in its former beauty and its former radiance. With the performance of this deed (on the part of God) nothing more was withheld from them. He still hid from them the divine power he had hidden from their ancestors.

According to chap. 46 (ibid.), even Alexander was impressed by the temple. The next Samaritan difficulties did not arise until the reign of Hadrian (cf. ibid., chap. 47).

[18]Yusuf b. Salama, Kafi, a MS. in the Gaster Collection of Samaritan Manuscripts of John Rylands Library in Manchester. It is concerned less with a development of the written law than with a handbook of the priestly knowledge about kosher butchering and about clean and unclean as well as about arguments which could be used against Jews and apparently even against dissenters inside the Samaritan community.

[19]*Ibid.*, chap. 18, "On the Pilgrimage to the Chosen Place".

[20]*Ibid.*

[21]*Ibid.*, chap. 4, "On Prayer".

[22]Gen. 28:17b.

[23]See above, note 7 (chap. II).

[24]Cf. Neubauer, *Chronique*, p. 403 (Bowman, *Tolidah*, p. 16 N).

[25]See above, chap. I, pp. 24-25.

[26]Vilmar, p. 82f. The "Adler Chronicle" (E. N. Adler und M. Séligsohn, "Une nouvelle chronique samaritaine," *Revue des Études Juives* 44 [1902], p. 188ff.; 45 [1902], p. 70ff., p. 223ff.; 46 [1903], p. 123ff.) transfers the appearance of the Dustan sect to the time of the high priesthood of Hanan and Hesekia, who were direct successors of Amram III, in whose reign the beginning of the sect was dated by Abu'l Fatḥ (*loc. cit.* 45 [1902], p. 72). While in the first reference to the Dustan sect Abu'l Fatḥ says nothing about the arch-heretic, he names Sara'ahu as its spiritual leader. The story is puzzling: Sara'ahu was the son of al Ra'is al Kabir, and had been relieved of his office because of a woman. When he saw that he no longer had a future inside the community (which community--the Samaritan or the Jewish?), he became the leader of the Dustan sect. It is significant that according to Abu'l Fatḥ, it was customary among the Dustan sect to count the fifty days until Pentecost "like the Jews from the morning of the Sabbath on". Similarities in matters of the calendar could point to the origin of this influence. Also significant is the statement, which is attributed

Notes to pp. 38-40

to them, that one had worshipped God in the land of Zuwaila, before he was worshipped on Mount Gerizim.

Saraʿahu is not the correct name of the priest of the Dustan sect. According to Abu'l Fatḥ, he received it in this way: "He composed a book in which he described all the high priests in a satirical manner, and indeed in a very clever manner, for in his time there was no one who was as learned as himself, and therefore we named him Saraʿahu" ("he sowed it" or "he brought it to blossom"). We ask ourselves whether Abu'l Fatḥ's story of the son of the high priest, who became the leader of the Dustan sect originated from Jaddua's son Manasseh, who married Sanballat's daughter and thereby turned out to be unfit in the eyes of Ezra's followers. Does Abu'l Fatḥ perhaps reject in this way the tradition of Sanballat's son-in-law who became a Samaritan high priest? For he could well be the high priest of the Dustan sect but not the high priest of the Samaritan community.

[27] Cf. Neubauer, Chronique, p. 404 (Bowman, Tolidah, p. 18).

[28] Cf. on the other hand Montgomery, Samaritans, p. 261.

[29] Vilmar, p. 151f.

[30] The story of Yahdu and his scruples against the eating of meat, in view of the end of the sacrificial service, is reminiscent of the story of Joshua ben Hananiah (Tos. Sota XV, 11 and T. B. B. Bat. 60b) who founded the Perushim, who would eat no meat, since as a result of the destruction of the temple in Jerusalem there was no more Tamid offering. Joshua proposed they should also drink no more wine, since there were also no more wine offerings.

[31] Epiphanius tells a similar story of the end of Dusis, Adv. Haer. I, 13.

[32] Vilmar, Abu'l Fatḥ, p. 156.

[33] Ant. 13:74-79.

[34] Vilmar, p. 102.

[35] Cf. Bowman, Ezekiel.

[36]See above, chap. IV, p. 102.

[37]Cf. J. Bowman, "Early Samaritan Eschatology," Journal of Jewish Studies 6 (1955), pp. 63-72; and Bowman, Ezekiel.

[38]The small Talmudic treatise about the Samaritans (Kuthim) concludes with the question: When would the Jews want to recognize the Samaritans? (Cf. Montgomery, Samaritans, p. 203).--Nothing is said against their theology of their faith in Moses, nor against the fact that they accepted only the Torah. Even in Judaism, Moses is the greatest prophet and the Torah is the most important part of the canon.--It was essential to the Jews only that the Samaritans give up the belief in Gerizim, recognize Zion, and confess the resurrection of the dead.

[39]Besides, the eschatology of 4th Ezra is occasionally identical to that of the Samaritans at a certain stage of development or of a Samaritan party, cf. especially 4 Ezra 7:26-30.

[40]See above, pp. 30-31.

[41]Cf. A. E. Cowley, The Samaritan Liturgy II, pp. 511-519.

[42]For a detailed discussion cf. J. Bowman, Early Samaritan Eschatology, loc. cit.

[43]Cf. Megillat Tan'anit I; T. B. Men. 65a on the date of Pentecost. Cf. M. Yad. IV, 7 with reference to the discussion among the Sadducees on the meaning of direct or indirect contact vis-a-vis the cause of impurity.

[44]Loc. cit., chap. 18: "The first day of Pesaḥ corresponds with the last day of Sukkoṯ." This refers to the route which the faithful cover up Mount Gerizim. On Pesaḥ and Sukkoṯ they only go up to Makkedah, on the Ḥagim (the seventh day of Maẓẓot, Shabu'ot, the first day of Sukkoṯ), on the other hand, they go up to the summit.

[45]Cf. Montgomery, Samaritans, p. 259: I consider "Ḳushtan" to be identical to Qusht (Truth), which is frequently used in the liturgy as a name for God (cf. ibid.).

Notes to pp. 43-46

[46]See above, chap. I, pp. 27, 39-40.

[47]If the "Sabbai" is actually related to the priestly nucleus, and if its name is really connected with a preference for the number seven, then the Samaritan assertion of the seven saints before Moses and the seven covenants in the Torah (cf. Montgomery, Samaritans, p. 232) can also be attributed to them. Even the calendar is published on the Sabbath days of the Ẓimmut, which is respectively seven Sabbath-days before the Passover and before the Feast of Tabernacles.

[48]Cf. Kafi, loc. cit., Chap. 18.

[49]The Samaritans burned the ashes of the Red Heifer up to the Middle Ages. Yusuf b. Salama reproached Rabbinic Judaism by saying that all its purity laws were null and void since they no longer burned the Red Heifer. Cf. J. Bowman, "Did the Qumran Sect Burn the Red Heifer?", Revue de Qumran 1 (1958), pp. 73-84.

[50]Cf. notes 26, 29 (chap. II) and p. 38 above.

[51]Vilmar, Abu'l Fatḥ, p. 82. According to the introduction to the Tolidah, the correct calendar calculation was a secret of the Samaritan high priest and was handed down from Adam to whom it was revealed by God. Edward Robertson, "Notes and Extracts from the Semitic MSS. in the John Rylands Library, Manchester, 6: The Astronomical Tables and Calendars of the Samaritans," Bulletin of the John Rylands Library 23 (1939), pp. 223-242, has pointed out that the Samaritans in the Middle Ages and afterwards used the al Battani charts.

[52]The Kafi of Yusuf b. Salama (cf. above, note 18 [chap. II]) is confined to issues of priestly interest, such as clean and unclean, calendar, pilgrimages, and sacrifices. Concerning impurity and the methods of purification, cf. chap. 10 which deals with leprosy as a special form of impurity. Leprosy first begins in the house, then comes the clothes, and finally it infects man. Later it is said that the basic reason for leprosy consists in evil gossip and false charges, the fall of Miriam is mentioned as an example. Chapter 12 contains the Samaritan priestly classification of the forms of impurity and statements

as to whether these can be eliminated by water or only by fire. Chapter 13 deals with impurity which cannot be eliminated by either one. In chapter 14, which deals with different kinds of impurities and the ways and means by which one receives them, it is stipulated that on the day a woman has her monthly impurity, she is fully absolved if she bathes before sunset. In addition, the _Kafi_ speak of a man who came and asked the high priest whether or not he would be unclean if he threw a stone over a grave. This priest answered him that a man who stepped over a grave would be unclean, but that it did not make him unclean if he threw a stone over it or if his shadow fell on a grave. The beginning of the _Kafi_ especially discusses in detail the question of reptiles in springs, as well as rules by which the water may be made pure if the reptile was removed.

[53]In the discussion on ritual slaughtering (_Shechita_) in chapter 30 the _Kafi_ does not mention eggs in a slaughtered bird, but states that an unborn calf may not be eaten. On the other hand, Yusuf b. Salama says in chapter 8: "Birds, which are to be eaten must be like the sacrifices destined for the altar." _Shechita_ and sacrifices appear to be identical to him. Eggs of birds which cannot be eaten (i.e. which are unsuitable as sacrificial animals) must also not be eaten. One could indeed assume that the prohibition of the Dustan sect against eating eggs (except for those which were found in slaughtered birds) originated from a concern for the preservation of the young and the species; but it is more likely that they really believed eggs must not be eaten unless they had been ritually slaughtered. This was naturally impossible. But if a hen had been ritually slaughtered, then the eggs in it would also be included in the sacrifice. The Dustan sect was, however, against sacrifice, as their abolition of the festivals shows. Could this attitude of the Dustan sect be indicative of vegetarianism? It is interesting that Shalya b. Tairun b. Nin evidentally insisted upon a vegetarian life (cf. below, p. 57).

[54]Cf. M. Ber. IX 5.

[55]J. Bowman, "Phylacteries," _Texte und Untersuchungen_, Transactions of the International Congress on the Four Gospels, Oxford, (1957).

Notes to pp. 47-49

[56]Vilmar, Abu'l Fatḥ, pp. 151-157. The members of this sect were obviously strict observers of the Sabbath. That appears to be the most important point in the Dusis sect. They did not go from one house to another, i.e. from one domain to another, on the Sabbath. Since they did not go from one house to another, they also carried nothing from one house to another, and therefore they recognized no ʿErub like the Samaritans of today. The sons of Yozadoq (a sect which was strongly influenced by the teaching of Dusis, cf. below, pp. 52-53) gave a special sanctity to all Sabbath days.

In the belief that earthenware vessels, which became ritually unclean on the Sabbath, could not be purified again, the Dustan sectarians are reminiscent of the strict sabbath-hallowing of the Damascus sect.

If the Dustan sectarians were unwilling to feed or water their cattle on the Sabbath, then they even surpassed the strict observance of the Sabbath by the Damascus sect. The latter at least permitted a man to graze his animals on the Sabbath, cf. C. Rabin, The Zadokite Documents (1954), p. 54.

[57]Until the Middle Ages, the Samaritans kept the Nazirite vow. We know from Yusuf b. Salama (loc. cit., chap. 19, "On the Nazirites"), that the Samaritan Nazirites kept their vows 373 days before they cut their hair at the conclusion of the vow.

[58]Vilmar, Abu'l Fatḥ, p. 82: "Children of the messenger (of God)."

[59]E. N. Adler and M. Seligsohn, loc. cit., p. 227.

[60]Vilmar, pp. 157-164; cf. E. N. Adler, etc., loc. cit., p. 231.

[61]Abu'l Fatḥ mentions another heretic, Ansma, but the story of Ansma and his disciples appears to be a duplication of his report on the Baʿunai.

[62]Vilmar, p. 160; E. N. Adler, etc., loc. cit., p. 231.

[63]Abu'l Fatḥ has all the sects die out.

[64]Vilmar, pp. 161-163.

[65]Probably the Tabernacle that disappeared at the end of the "Time of Divine Favour" under the high priesthood of Uzzi. (Cf. the Samaritan Book of Joshua, Th. W. J. Juynboll, _loc. cit._, chap. 42, about the cloud of darkness which covered the house and how it suggested to him to hide his clothing and the holy vessels in a cave. After he had done that he could no longer find the cave.)

[66]Cf. the way in which Pilate dealt with the Samaritan agitator who claimed to know where the holy vessels were hidden, Josephus, _Ant_. 18:85-87.

[67]Frequent immersions were probably a characteristic action of the Dositheans. Abu'l Fatḥ reports that the Dusis sect prayed in water: Vilmar, p. 157.

[68]Abu'l Fatḥ (or his source) speaks of Shalya, who neglected the ascension of Gerizim in which he followed Dusis. Dustan read "Elohim" instead of the Tetragrammaton, cf. _ibid_., p. 82.

[69]"The Friends": as I understand the Arabic (really Persian) expression "_al_ _Dustan_", _ibid_., p. 162. The use of this expression by one of the Dusis sects shows the close relationship, if not actual identity, of Dositheanism with the earlier Dustan sect. That he did not want to die on a Sabbath shows the great holiness which one generally conferred on the Sabbath as the only remaining festival.

[70]_Ibid_., p. 163.

[71]The Sons of Yozadoq agreed in this with Shalya and his sect. It was the Dustan sect who first threw out the "forever"; see above, p. 47.

[72]The latter stands in contrast to Shalya's attitude, see above.

[73]Cf. Montgomery, _Samaritans_, p. 255ff.

Notes to p. 54

[74]The author does not deny that there is a belief in angels among the Samaritans of today. However it is significant that Epiphanius testifies to their rejection of the belief in angels (Adv. Haer. IX, 13). Significantly in the Kitab al-Tabah of Hassan al-Suri, a priestly work of the 11th century, the writer in the section about angels does not take the verse of the Torah in which the "Angel of the Lord" is mentioned as a proof text for the existence of angels. The older Samaritanism made a strenuous effort to attribute all glory to God alone, cf. Gen. 48:16 where the Samaritan text does not read "angel" but "king", i.e. God.

In his section about angels, Abu'l Hassan mentions only one angel's name: Kabod (Glory). Abu'l Hassan's teaching about the angels rests above all on the Pentateuch. Therefore it is interesting to see which passages he used and which passages he ignored in order to prove the existence of angels. He passes over, for example, Gen. 3:24, the cherubim at the door to the garden of Eden, and does not quote Gen. 19:1 about the two angels who went to Sodom. He mentions neither Gen. 32:2 on the angels of God, who met Jacob en route, nor Gen. 48:16 where Jacob called on the angel to bless Ephraim and Manasseh. He also does not appeal to the "angel of the Lord" in the Exodus and wilderness wandering stories. The texts he does use are: Ex. 24:17: "And at the appearance of the glory of the Lord it was like a burning fire on the peak of the mountain in the eyes of the children of Israel"; Ex. 24:10: "And they saw the God of Israel. Under his feet it was like a beautiful Sapphire." (In the Samaritan Targum it is said: "And they feared the God of Israel, and there where they met him the ground was like a Sapphire.") The "God of Israel" could not be called "God" here according to Abu'l Hassan, but "angel", for man has not seen God. He used this verse in order to prove that angels have feet, precisely just as he used Num. 22:31--where Balaam sees the angel of God with a sword in his hand--in order to show that angels can stand and have hands. He uses Gen. 1:2 about the Spirit of God which hovered over the water in order to show that angels have wings. When he quotes Num. 12:8: "And he saw the form of the Lord", then "Lord" here means not "God" but "angel" for him.

[75]Although the "Word" of Yahweh is found in Num. 22:20; 23:4, 5, 16.

[76]Cf. J. Bowman, "The Exegesis of the Pentateuch among the Samaritans and among the Rabbis," Oudtestamentische Studiën 8 (1950), pp. 220-262, and also concerning the pre-existence of Moses and his ascension.

[77]Abu'l Hassan, Kitab al-Tabaḥ, chap. 16 ("and he died").

[78]Cf. J. Bowman, "The Doctrine of Creation, Fall of Man, and Original Sin in Samaritan and Pauline Theology," The Reformed Theological Review 19 (1960), p. 65.

[79]This idea is also found in the Molad Moshe and in the Asatir. Clearly the Malef, like the Molad Moshe, is dependent on the Asatir. But the Asatir is without doubt an old Dosithean work. Perhaps in the Molad Moshe part of the birth-story is given to us, which is no longer contained in the Memar Marqah since the first book is missing.

[80]In J. W. Nutt, Fragments of a Samaritan Targum, with an Introduction (1874), p. 69, note 1, it is mentioned that J. H. Petermann had heard from a Samaritan priest, that the "Spirit of God" and "darkness" in Gen. 1 meant the good and evil angels. The names of the four most important angels were Phanuel (Gen. 32:31), Anusa (Ex. 14:25), Kabbala' (Num. 4:20) and Nasi (Ex. 17:15). The devils were 'Azazel (Lev. 16:8ff.), Belial (Deut. 15:9), and Gasara (perhaps the "hornets" of Ex. 23:28). The descendants of Cain were evil spirits; the Nephilim (Gen. 6:4) are likewise evil angels, who fell from heaven.

Clearly the report of the priest in reference to the resurrection was conflicting. At one time he said that the spirits of good and evil men would recover their bodies in the last judgement and would enter with them either into paradise or into hell; at another time he explained they would always remain in a bodiless state.

[81]The "Children of Light and Darkness" in I QS IV is especially striking. Cf. below, chap. IV, p. 82.

[82]Cf. Epiphanius, Adv. Haer. VIII.

Notes to p. 57

Notes to Chapter III

"The Samaritans and the Gospel"

[1]In M. Dem. III, 4 the Samaritans are not treated as heathens, but as Jewish 'Am ha 'areẓ. But M. Dem. V, 9 makes a distinction between an Israelite and a Samaritan. However a distinction is also made between a Samaritan and a pagan. Their attitude towards the Samaritans was therefore not always the same. So one finds, for example, in T. B. Ber. 47b the opinion that the Samaritans keep the written law and that in what they observe they are stricter than the Jews. On the other hand, M. Shebi. V111, 10 says that to eat the bread the Samaritans eat is the same as eating pork.

[2]The precise term reads as follows: "Books standing outside" (Sepharim ha-ḥizonim) M. Sanh. X, 1. Here R. 'Akibah numbers those who read the "non-canonical books" with those Israelites who have no share in the world to come. One could argue, and it would be perfectly natural to do so, that 'Akibah, who was decisively interested in the acceptance of the Songs of Solomon into the canon (cf. M. Yad. III, 5), wished to stress in this indirect way the importance of canonical writings. However, it could be assumed that ḥizonim is a word for "heretic" and that the name "Essene" could have originated from it, since it should be remembered that the beginning het-sound, like all guttural sounds, was not pronounced by the Samaritans. Therefore are the Sepharim ha-ḥizonim "non-canonical" or "Essene books"? The fact that in T. B. Sanh. 100b our term was apparently understood in a wider sense does not completely speak against the second possibility, since that may reflect a completely later usage.

[3]One is amazed to find here a friendly interest in the ten lost tribes, e.g. 2 Bar. 1:2 (the lost nine and one half tribes), 2 Bar. 77:19 and 78:1 (the return of the ten tribes), cf. also 4 Ezra 13:40-48. In this connection one especially thinks of the Testament of the Twelve Patriarchs and its discovery in the caves of Qumran.

Notes to pp. 57-58

[4]Cf. in addition: J. Bowman, "Samaritan Studies I. The Fourth Gospel and the Samaritans," Bulletin of the John Rylands Library 40 (1958), pp. 299f.

[5]Acts 1:8: "And you will be my witnesses to Jerusalem and all Judea and Samaria and to the ends of the earth." Cf. also Acts 8:1, 5, 9, 14; 9:31; 15:3.

[6]Cf. Acts 8:14, 25.

[7]Lk. 17:18.

[8]Acts 15:7. One should not forget Acts 10:17 with the Cornelius story and Acts 11:17 with Peter's defense of his deeds: "Who was I, that I could withstand God?" Does this refer to only this event?

[9]The Simon-Magus story in Acts 8:19-25 is significant. According to Abu'l Fatḥ (cf. Vilmar, p. 157) Simon clearly appears to have been numbered among the Dusis sect; for here he is mentioned directly after the report about the Dusis sect and prior to the one about the Baʿunai, who were clearly identified as disciples of Dusis (ibid., p. 159). Simon is "the magician from ʿAlin". According to one report, Simon was willing to kill the son of the Samaritan high priest. Abu'l Fatḥ says (ibid.):

> And Simon was humiliated before the high priest and went away immediately and retired to Armiya (Rome). And he and the followers of the messiah practiced magic; but he was the master of them all. Then he found a Jewish philosopher in Alexandria with the name of Philo, and he (Simon) said: 'Strengthen me, and I will put an end to the sect of the messiah.' Philo said to him: 'Be calm, for if this thing originated from God (cf. Acts 5:39), no one has the power to bring it to an end.' So Simon turned back and went to Beit ʿAlin and died and was buried in the wadi opposite the house of the disciple, who had first borne witness of the messiah, and his name was Saftana (Stephen). And there were fifteen disciples of the messiah, the last of whom was Jude and the circumcised disciples were assigned to him. And from then on they no longer admitted circumcised ones for all were un-circumcised.

Notes to pp. 59-69

[10]Samaritan Studies I. "The Fourth Gospel and the Samaritans," Bulletin of the John Rylands Library 40 (1958), pp. 298-308.

[11]Cf. ibid., pp. 302ff. This Samaritan doctrine originates from the Malef, cf. above, p. 55. Cf. now the whole work of J. MacDonald, The Theology of the Samaritans (1964).

[12]Not, as it is interpreted by Jews and Christians, "like one of us". For the Samaritan, Moses is the "one from him" who knew good and evil.

[13]According to the story of the Fall, as it is told in Pirke de R. Eliezer 31 (G. Friedlaender, loc. cit., p. 105f.) Sammael seduced Eve using the snake as a mediator, and from this sexual offense Cain and Abel were born; it is emphasized that it can only be said of Seth, but not of Cain and Abel, that Adam had procreated him in his image. The Samaritan story of the Fall does not mention the seduction of Eve by Belial; however, the sons of Cain are characterized as sons of Belial.

[14]Luke 1:5 "a certain priest named Zechariah from the order of Abijah"; Luke 1:9ff. "Zechariah in the Temple"; Luke 24:53: "And they (the disciples) were always in the Temple, glorifying and praising God."

[15]Cf., e.g. the purification of Mary and the delivery of her first born (2:22-24), the recognition of the messiah by Simeon, the Hasid, in the Temple (2:25f.), the Passover in Jerusalem, when Jesus was twelve years old and sat in the Temple among the scribes (2:41-46), the Temptation of Jesus, when Satan put Jesus on the pinnacle of the Temple (4:9). (In the gospel of Matthew, the Temple is mentioned for the first time in connection with the Temptation story [4:5]). In Luke 5:14 and 17:14, the lepers are commanded to show themselves to the high priest. The leper is told in 5:14: "Go show yourself to the priest and sacrifice for your cleansing, as Moses commanded in witness thereto." In 17:14 it is said of the ten lepers in the pericope: "Go and show yourselves to the priests. And it happened that as they went, they were cleansed." In 17:15f. is mentioned the one leper who turned around and showed himself to Jesus. This former

leper was a Samaritan. Is the Samaritan reader to be shown in this way that Jesus was recognized and acknowledged as a priest by a Samaritan?

[16]Luke 9:52-56.

[17]Luke 10:30ff.

[18]Cf. J. Bowman, "The Parable of the Good Samaritan," _Expository Times_ 59 (1948), p. 151f. and "Further Note on the Parable of the Good Samaritan," _ibid_., p. 243. The conclusion of the small tractate _Kuthim_ (cf. above, chapter II, note 38) assumes that only the Jews were Israelites for the Rabbis.

[19]Cf. above, note 15.

[20]Luke 16:16.

[21]_Kafi_, _loc_. _cit_., chap. 4.

[22]Cf. Bowman, _Ezekiel_.

[23]1 Chron. 24:4ff.

[24]Cf. 1 Chron. 24:10 where Abijah is counted as the eighth order. If according to 24:4 the first 16 orders were Zadokite, then Abijah would belong to them.

[25]Cf. J. Bowman, "Is the Samaritan Calendar the Old Zadokite One?", _Palestine Exploration Quarterly_ 91 (1959), pp. 23-37. Cf. above, Chap. II, pp. 42-43.

[26]Probably not until the end of the first century B.C. did one begin to implement strictly and in every detail the doctrine of the two Torahs--one transmitted in writing, the other orally--but both having Mosaic origins.

[27]Cf. the "historical haggadah" about John Hyrcanus T. B. Qid. 66a (cf. Josephus, _Ant_. 13, 288ff.). That is only told in order to underscore a halakic viewpoint, namely whether one or two men are necessary to give evidence.

Notes to pp. 74-78

[28]Ezek. 44:20 in any case says of the priests: "Your head should not be shaved and the hair is also not to be permitted to grow freely but should be cropped round about." But Yusuf b. Salama says in the _Kafi_ (_loc_. _cit_., chap. 19, "On the Nazirites") that a Nazirite can let his hair grow _and_ cut it; the hair of the high priests is never cut.

[29]M. Naz. I, 7.

[30]M. Naz. I, 3.

[31]Cf. Num. 6:14.

[32]Josephus, _Ant_. 19, 294; M. Naz. II, 5f.; cf. Acts 21:24-26.

[33]Cf. _loc_. _cit_., Chapter 19, "On the Nazarites," also in the following. On the rules of Yusuf b. Salama on the Nazirites, cf. in addition J. Bowman, "The Importance of Samaritan Researches," _The Annual of Leeds University Oriental Society_ I (1959), p. 52f.

[34]Here is meant the _me nidda_ which the Samaritans obtained from the ashes of the red heifer until the late Middle Ages.

[35]Cf. J. van Goudoever, _Biblical Calendars_ (1959), p. 272ff.

[36]The sabbatical year began, like the year of Jubilees, with Tisḥri the 7th month of the festival year in which the Sukkoṯ (Feast of Tabernacles) was celebrated. On the beginning of the year of Jubilees, cf. Lev. 25:9; on the beginning of the year of release, cf. Deut. 31:10.

[37]For more about it see above (_op_. _cit_.) note 25.

[38]For an example of the Sabbath Sheḳalim see Ex. 30:1-10; Sabbath Zaḵor, Deut. 25:17-19; Sabbath Parah, Num. 19:1-22; Ha-Kodesh [Passover], Ex. 12:1-20.

[39]Cf. above, note 27.

[40]Luke 1:17.

[41]Cf. above (_op_. _cit_.) note 25.

Notes to pp. 79-81

[42]Luke 1:69. On the following cf. 1:68-79, especially verses 73 and 76.

[43]This is the only angel's name which is mentioned in Abu'l Hassan. Montgomery, *Samaritans*, p. 219, mentions four names: *Kabbala'*, *Pennuel*, *Anusa*, and *Silpa*. *Kabbala'* is also named as an angel in the Leeds Bishop Samaritan Phylactery No. 2, as well as *Silpa*.

[44]It is remarkable that the Shekinah is actually called the *Kabod* in Ezekiel. On the splendour of the Lord which rises from the temple, see Ezek. 9:3 and 10:4f. On the glory of the Lord which comes back to Ezekiel's new temple, see Ezek. 44:4.

[45]Luke 2:14: the goodwill which falls on the men is from God. Cf. Isa. 61:2: "to proclaim a merciful year of the Lord," i.e. the Year of Divine Favour.

[46]Cf. the Samaritan Book of Joshua, chapter 42 (Th. W. J. Juynboll, *loc. cit.*).

[47]The Sabbath of the Mofetim, see A. E. Cowley, *loc. cit.*, pp. 284-334.

[48]That is shown by the full name of the *Tolidah*: *Shalshelet ha-kohanim me-'Adam 'ad ha-yom*. There is a parallel between the ancestors of Jesus, who lived before the Flood and the "priests" in the *Tolidah* who lived before the Flood. This may be especially indicative, if one considers that Charles in his edition of Jubilees points out the similarity between the era before the Flood in the book of Jubilees and in the *Tolidah* (cf. above, chapter I, p. 13). The *Tolidah* has points of contact throughout with the Zadokite tradition, e.g. with the Zadokite priestly genealogy of 1 Chron. 5:27-41. The Jubilees are also connected in some way with the Zadokite tradition, as is attested by the calendar of the book of Jubilees in connection with the calendar of the Qumran sect (see below, p. 116). As we have seen, Luke is interested in the priestly position. Perhaps he wanted to please the Jerusalem as well as the Shechem/Nablus Zadokites.

[49]Ezek. 37:25; cf. J. Bowman, "Early Samaritan Eschatology," *Journal of Jewish Studies* 6 (1955), p. 63f.

Notes to pp. 81-89

[50]Cf. Bowman, _Ezekiel_, p. 13.

[51]Genesis 50:13.

[52]It is explained similarly in the gospel of Luke that the day of Law is past, although it, as long as it was in force, had to be fulfilled. The Samaritans certainly agreed with all their hearts that the Jews had never kept the Law and had changed it.

[53]The "Scribes" were probably priestly scholars about whom, however, the rabbinic sources make incorrect statements, since they claimed to have been more authoritative than they were in reality in the time before 70 A.D.

[54]The prophet who is like Moses (cf. Deut. 18:18) appears in the book of Acts not only in the defensive speech of Stephen but also in the speeches of Peter (e.g. 3:22).

[55]Justin Martyr, _Apol_. I, 26.56; II, 15.

[56]Cf. above, note 1.

[57]Originally I was persuaded on the basis of my study of the Samaritan liturgy and the Malef that the gospel of John, although it stresses that salvation comes from the Jews, still wanted to present Christ and his teaching in a way which would be understandable to Samaritanism in general. Since then, I have recognized that Dosithean teachings are also found in the Samaritan hymns and other texts of the sixteenth century and afterwards which would have originally been unacceptable to the Samaritan priesthood; I think that we must take into account more seriously the schism which existed so long in Samaritanism. Therefore I now connect the gospel of John to the Dositheans alone.

Notes to Chapter IV

"The Samaritans and the Sect of Qumran"

[1]See above, chap. II, pp. 43-44.

[2]See above, chap. I, p. 14.

[3]See above, chap. I, pp. 27-28.

[4]Cf. Vilmar, Abu'l Fatḥ, pp. 151-157, Epiphanius, Adv. haer., XIII, 1. Excerpts from Makrisi, Masudi and Shahrastani can be found in S. de Sacy, Chrestomathie Arabe (1826).

[5]He reports at the beginning of his work (cf. Vilmar) that in the year 1352 A.D. he had been authorized by the present high priest Phineas to write an official history of the Samaritans. Phineas even placed the sources at his [Abu'l Fatḥ's] disposal, and Abu'l Fatḥ says: "They are in the present wording." Abu'l Fatḥ's historical work was not only written in order to arouse in the Samaritans pride in their history, but also in order to show them that they are real heirs of the best of the past. That he could make use of the Samaritan Book of Joshua in it, which--as we have seen (see above, Chap. I, p. 17f.)--is a Dosithean work, shows that at his time the schism had been overcome. However, that the Dositheans are treated in his work as a sect, on the other hand, does not prove much. It signifies only that one who was authorized by a high priest supported orthodoxy as opposed to the heresies, with regard to the time in which they were still real heresies.

[6]Cf. the Joshua Book, chaps. 23 and 24 (Th. W. J. Juynboll, loc. cit.).

[7]Cf. above, chap. II, pp. 46-47, 50-51.

[8]Cf. Jos., Ant. 13, 74-79; Dam. V, 11.

[9]Dam. V, 8; T. B. B Bat. 115b.

Notes to pp. 94-100

[10] See above, chap. II, p. 55f.

[11] See above, chap. I, p. 13.

[12] For example in the hymns of ʿAbdalla b. Solomon, the most prolific author of the 14th century (on him cf. now J. Macdonald, _The Theology of the Samaritans_ [1964], _passim_), who appears to have played an important role in the renewal of the liturgy of reunited Samaritanism, a liturgy in which the hymns and prayers in the synagogue at the time of high festivals take the place of the pilgrimage to the holy mountain. Up until the 14th century, the Samaritan liturgy, which originated on the whole from the 4th century, was not very extensive, but then it was very much expanded. In this new liturgical creation, views are integrated throughout which were previously held only by the Dositheans (cf. J. Bowman, "The Importance of Samaritan Researches," _The Annual of Leeds University Oriental Society_ 1 [1959], p. 49).

[13] W. H. Brownlee, _The Dead Sea Manual of Discipline, Translation and Notes_ (Bulletin of the American Schools of Oriental Research [1951] Supplementary Studies 10-12), _loc. cit_.

[14] 1 QS III, 19. One could also translate _toledot ha-'emet_ with "the ones who were born in the truth" and _toledot ha-ʿavel_ with "the ones who were born in depravity--or in deceit".

[15] Cf. above, chap. II, note 79, p. 135.

[16] The Marqah hymns, although they are now orthodox, could have originally been used for the service in Baba's new synagogue. Marqah had teachings in his hymns and _Memar_ which are not contained in Abu'l Hassan's _Kitab al-Tabah_ (11th century) and which first appeared again in the reunified Samaritanism of the 14th century and later.

[17] Cf. above, chap. II, p. 55; chap. III, p. 63-65.

[18] Cf. above, chap. III, p. 63f.

[19] See above, chap. II, p. 49.

[20]In addition, requests were uttered in their prayer "for the salvation of Moses". Cf. A. E. Cowley, The Samaritan Liturgy (1909), I, p. 62ff.

[21]See above, chap. II, p. 49.

[22]The word "way" is used both in Qumran and Luke in the sense of "teaching". Cf. for example 1 QS IX, 17 and Acts 9:2; 24:14.

[23]Cf. 1 QS III, 13-IV, 26; V, 20f.

[24]Dam. VII, 20.

[25]The earliest Samaritan temple built on Mount Gerizim was that of Sanballat, which was destroyed by Hyrcanus.

[26]Cf. 1 QS I, 16-II, 18.

[27]Deut. 27f. The Samaritan community climbed in a procession to the holy mountain at Mazzot, Shabu'ot and Sukkot (cf. MS 1111 of the Gaster Collection of Samaritan Manuscripts in the John Rylands Library in Manchester). The procession began at the house of the priest at the foot of the mountain, where the Torah passage Gen. 33:18 (Jacob's entry into Shechem) is recited in qaṭaf form (for the Qeṭafim cf. J. Bowman, "Samaritan Studies III, Samaritan Law and Liturgy," Bulletin of the John Rylands Library 40 [1958], pp. 322-327), while on the slope of the mountain the blessings and curses in Deut. 27f. were recited word for word.

[28]E.g. 1 QS V, 24-VI, 25, etc. 1 QS IX, 21 will show that the author or editor of the great part of the Manual of Discipline considered it to be halakah. As an example of the halakic part of the Damascus Document, cf. the laws concerning the Sabbath: X, 14-XI, 18; concerning impurity: XII, 1f., 9-19; concerning bathing: X, 10f.

[29]Cf. J. Bowman, "Contact between Samaritan Sects and Qumran?", Vetus Testamentum 7 (1957), pp. 184-189.

Notes to pp. 104-108

[30]At least in the 11th century, when Yusuf b. Salama wrote, they still existed. Yusuf maintained there could be Nazirites, as long as a high priest and purification were available.

[31]Cf. in addition and on the following: Yusuf b. Salama, *Kafi*, *loc. cit.*, chap. 19, "On the Nazirites", and above, chap. III, p. 75.

[32]Cf. above, chap. II, pp. 38-39. Dusis met Yahdu, a learned Samaritan, as he ate the firstborn and asked him in reference to Num. 18:17: "Is it not a violation of the Law, if one eats the firstborn whose blood has not been sprinkled on the altar?" Yahdu answered: "And it is like the bread of which God said: 'And you should eat neither bread nor grain, neither roasted nor fresh.' And they ceased to eat the bread and firstborn for two years." Later they ate and drank and became drunk (Vilmar, *Abu'l Fath*, p. 151). Obviously they drank nothing for two years.

[33]The Mishnah reports of Queen Helena that she lived as a Nazirite for 21 years (M. Naz. III, 6).

[34]Cf. *loc. cit.*, chap. 1, "On the Priesthood".

[35]See above, chap. II, p. 46.

[36]Yusuf b. Salama wrote at a time when the Dositheans still formed a uniform group among the Samaritans.

[37]Cf. above, chap. I, p. 13.

[38]Cf. 1 QS VI, 16f., 20; Josephus *Bell*. 2, 137f.

[39]So I interpret "A share in the purity of the Many". *Me nidda* were basically for the observance of the law of purity.

[40]*Loc. cit.*, chap. 19, "On the Nazirites".

[41]"Did the Qumran Sect Burn the Red Heifer?", *Revue de Qumran* 1 (1958), pp. 73-84; see there also concerning the following.

[42]Josephus, Bell. 2, 129f.

[43]Cf. M. Ḥag. II, 7.

[44]1 QS III, 4.

[45]Num. 19:3.

[46]Even in Rabbinic Judaism, in which the laity were considered to be just as good as the priests, only priests could offer sacrifices and although the Pharaisaic laity could and even did keep the priestly laws of purification, for their part that was only a work of supererogation. As M. Ḥag II, 2 shows, if a layman could observe in the greatest detail all the ritual laws of purification he could not come close to a priest who could handle the me nidda, let alone prepare it himself.

[47]Lev. 23:2.

[48]See above, chap. II, pp. 42-43.

[49]If the creation myths were received and retouched by the author of the priestly writing [i.e. "P"], then the Jewish priests who came home from Babylon to Jerusalem must have also brought along some knowledge of the calendar. In any case, they brought with them the new names of the months.

[50]Ezek. 5:5; 38:12.

[51]M. R. ha-Sh. II, 8f.

[52]M. R. ha-Sh. I, 7; II, 5.

[53]Cf. M. Taʿan, IV, 5.

[54]Cf. Vilmar, p. 82.

[55]That amounts to the same thing; for when one changes the times of the festivals, one declares at the same time that all the festivals which are not celebrated on the newly established days are invalid.

Notes to pp. 115-116

[56]See above, chap. II, p. 44.

[57]As I understand 1 QS X, 3ff.

[58]Concerning the Samaritans, this was very clear from the _Tolidah_. It was also noted in the _Memar Marqah_. On the significance of Pentecost in the Book of Jubilees, see Jub. 6:17f.

[59]Cf. 1 QS X, 3 and J. Bowman, "Is the Samaritan Calendar the Old Zadokite One?", _Palestine Exploration Quarterly_ 91 (1959). It is significant that Jesus Sirach (50:6f.) in his great eulogy for the high priest Simon compares him with the sun and moon. That may be poetic speech, but it can also be applied to the function of the high priest concerning the calendar. So Moses and Aaron are also compared with the sun and moon (cf. A. D. Cowley, _loc. cit._, I, p. 100). Even more interesting in this connection is the passage (_ibid._, p. 106) where the emphasis is placed on the fundamental necessity of the priestly knowledge of the sun and moon for religion and life.

ABBREVIATED REFERENCES CITED IN THE NOTES

Bowman, *Ezekiel*.................. J. Bowman, "Ezekiel and the Zadokite Priesthood". *Transactions of the Glasgow University Oriental Society* 16 (1955/56), 1-14.

Bowman, *Tolidah*.................. J. Bowman, *Transcript of the Original Text of the Samaritan Chronicle Tolidah* (1954).

Gaster, *Samaritans*................ M. Gaster, *The Samaritans. Their History, Doctrines, and Literature*. (The Schweich Lectures 1923) (1925).

Montgomery, *Samaritans*........... J. A. Montgomery, *The Samaritans, the Earliest Jewish Sect. Their History, Theology and Literature* (1907).

Neubauer, *Chronique*.............. A. Neubauer, "Chronique samaritaine suivie d'un Appendice contenant de courtes notices sur quelques autres ouvrages samaritains". *Journal Asiatique* series 6, 14 (1869), 385-470.

Vilmar, *Abu'l Fath*................ *Abulfathi Annales samaritani quos ad fidem codicum manuscriptorum Berolinensium, Bodlejani, Parisini edidit et prolegomenis instruxit* Eduardus Vilmar (1865).

For a bibliography on the Samaritans, cf. now L. A. Mayer, *Bibliography of the Samaritans*, ed. by D. Broadribb (Supplements to Abr-Nahrain I, edited by J. Bowman) Leiden (1964).

A SELECTED BIBLIOGRAPHY OF ADDITIONAL WORKS BY JOHN BOWMAN ON THE SAMARITANS

1. "The Parable of the Good Samaritan". _Expository Times_ 59 (6, 1948), pp. 151-153.

2. "The Parable of the Good Samaritan: Additional Note". _Expository Times_ 59 (9, 1948), pp. 248-249.

3. "The Leeds Samaritan Decalogue Inscription". _Proceedings of the Leeds Philosophical Society_ 6 (1951), pp. 567-575.

4. "The Exegesis of the Pentateuch among the Samaritans and among the Rabbis". _Oudtestamentische Studiën_ 8 (1950), pp. 220-262.

5. "Samaritan Decalogue Inscriptions". _Bulletin of the John Rylands Library_ 33 (1951), pp. 211-236.

6. _Transcript of the Original Text of the Samaritan Chronicle Tolidah_ (with a critical introduction). Mimeographed. University of Leeds: Dept. of Semitic Languages, 1954. [This transcript is available from the Yale University Library.]

7. _The Hebrew Text of a Samaritan Allegory by Phinehas on the Taheb_. University of Leeds: Dept. of Semitic Languages, 1955.

8. "Early Samaritan Eschatology". _Journal of Jewish Studies_ 6 (2, 1955), pp. 63-72.

9. "Ezekiel and the Zadokite Priesthood". _Transactions of the Glasgow University Oriental Society_ 16 (1955/56), pp. 1-14.

10. "Contact between Samaritan Sects and Qumran?" _Vetus Testamentum_ 7 (1957), pp. 184-189.

11. "Phylacteries". Texte und Untersuchungen zur Geschichte der Altchristlichen Literatur 73 (1959), pp. 523-538.

12. "Phylacteries". Transactions of the Glasgow University Oriental Society 15 (1957), pp. 54-55.

13. "The Samaritans and the Book of Deuteronomy". Transactions of the Glasgow University Oriental Society 17 (1957-58), pp. 9-18.

14. "Samaritan Studies I, II, III". Bulletin of the John Rylands Library 40 (2, 1958), pp. 298-327. Including:
I. "The Fourth Gospel and the Samaritans", pp. 298-308.
II. "Faith in Samaritan Thought", pp. 308-315.
III. "Samaritan Law and Liturgy", pp. 315-327.
This series of articles has also been reprinted as a monograph with the title: Samaritan Studies. Manchester, England: Manchester University Press, 1958.

15. "Did the Qumran Sect Burn the Red Heifer?" Revue de Qumran 1 (1958), pp. 73-84.

16. "Is the Samaritan Calendar the Old Zadokite One?" Palestine Exploration Quarterly 91 (1959), pp. 23-37.

17. "The Importance of Samaritan Researches". The Annual of Leeds University Oriental Society 1 (1958/59), pp. 43-54.

18. "An Interesting Leningrad Samaritan Manuscript". Abr-Nahrain 1 (1959), pp. 73-78.

19. "The Doctrine of Creation, Fall of Man and Original Sin in Samaritan and Pauline Theology". The Reformed Theological Review 19 (3, 1960), pp. 65-72.

20. "Pilgrimage to Mount Gerizim". Eretz-Israel 7 (1963), pp. 17-28.

21. "The Identity and Date of the Unnamed Feast of John 5:1" in Near Eastern Studies in Honor of William Foxwell Albright. ed. Hans Goedicke. Baltimore/London: The John Hopkins Press, 1971, pp. 43-56.

22. "Teshubah". Abr-Nahrain 15 (1975). Forthcoming. At the end of this study, materials relevant to the Samaritan doctrine of the Taheb will be presented.

23. Encyclopaedia and dictionary articles by John Bowman:

    (1) "Samaritans". Dictionary of the Bible. 2nd ed. (original edition by James Hastings). Revised by F. C. Grant and H. H. Rowley. Edinburgh: T. & T. Clark, 1963, p. 880.

    (2) "Samaritans". Standard Jewish Encyclopaedia. ed. Cecil Roth. New York: Doubleday, 1959, p. 1647.

TRANSLATOR'S NOTE

Throughout the preceeding body of the text one will find page references in brackets, e.g. [p.50] on p. 53. The numbers in these brackets refer to the original pagination of the German edition. This was done to help those readers wishing to cite the original German pagination or to compare the English and German editions.

In the indices which follow, numbers in parenthesis, e.g. (80), refer to footnotes. The page on which that footnote appears immediately precedes it, e.g. 135 (80) = p. 135, n. 80. Furthermore, a few minor errors were detected in the indices of the German edition (from which these indices were taken), which have been corrected. One will note that in the index on Josephus one page number appears in brackets. This was also found in the index to the German edition. The reason for this peculiarity seems to be that Dr. Bowman refers to this passage from Josephus (*Ant*. 13, 74-79) on p. 43 [Eng. ed.], although he does not explicitly cite it either in the text or the footnote that follows.

The German edition originally had its footnotes at the bottom of each page. To simplify typing and expedite publication, however, we have chosen to place these notes at the end of the book. To facilitate the process of referring back and forth between the text and footnotes, we have included the page numbers of the text to which these notes refer on the top of each note page. Furthermore, in the indices which follow, whenever a reference is given both in the text itself and in a footnote, both the pagination of the text and the footnote are given. If the reference appears only in the footnote, then only the page number of that note appears. I trust this brief explanation and these additions will lessen the labor of the reader.

Alfred M. Johnson, Jr.

I. INDEX TO BIBLICAL PASSAGES

A. Old Testament

B. New Testament

LUKE (cont.)

JOHN

ACTS

1 CORINTHIANS

II. INDEX TO NONCANONICAL LITERATURE

A. Apocrypha and Pseudepigrapha (Old Testament)

B. Samaritan Literature

C. Josephus

D. Rabbinical Writings

E. Qumran Writings

III. AUTHORS CITED

SÉLIGSOHN, M.

See the Adler Chronicle under II.B. above.

BEN SOLOMON, ʿABDALLA

See the Hymns under II.B. above.

SPIRO, A.

126 (16).

VILMAR, E.

See the Annals of Abu'l Fatḥ under II.B. above.